Elena Desanta

OrangeBooks Publication

1st Floor, Rajhans Arcade, Mall Road, Kohka, Bhilai, Chhattisgarh 490020

Website:**www.orangebooks.in**

© Copyright, 2024, Author

All rights reserved. No part of this book may be reproduced, stored in a retrieval system, or transmitted, in any form by any means, electronic, mechanical, magnetic, optical, chemical, manual, photocopying, recording or otherwise, without the prior written consent of its writer.

First Edition, 2024

ISBN: 978-93-6554-115-1

Elena DeSanta

Shadows and Light: Navigating through Complexities of life

YASH BHAVSAR

OrangeBooks Publication
www.orangebooks.in

"Dear Reader" is a reflection of Yash's own path of self-discovery and his study of the human spirit, rather than merely a memoir of the fictional Elena DeSanta. As a young writer, Yash extends an invitation to readers to join him on a trip that, despite his own particular struggles and victories, speaks to everyone who has ever tried to blaze their own trail through life's turmoil.

Yash has created a story that explores deep life themes while also appreciating the small pleasures of daily life, all while juggling his love of writing and his academic obligations. His first literary endeavour is an engaging read because of his storytelling method, which is characterised by empathy and insight frequently found in seasoned writers.

With his debut, Yash not only proves himself as an engineering student but also as a perceptive and thoughtful storyteller who is sure to leave a lasting impression on both the literary world and his readers.

Contents

Chapter - 0
Roots and Crossroads 1

Chapter - 1
Foundations and Relations 5

Chapter - 2
Embracing the Majesty of Drakensberg 11

Chapter - 3
Embracing Family and Community 16

Chapter - 4
The Tapestry of New Beginnings 20

Chapter - 5
Echoes of Discord 28

Chapter - 6
Unfamiliar Feelings 35

Chapter - 7
Embracing Womanhood 39

Chapter - 8
Departing Echoes 44

Chapter - 9
Shadows of Betrayal 48

Chapter - 10
Unveiling Miguel's Secret Surfing 53

Chapter - 11
Blossoming Friendship 56

Chapter – 12
    Exploring California's Wonders 63

Chapter – 13
    Jake's Departure: A Bittersweet Adieu 68

Chapter – 14
    A New Rival, A New Friend 73

Chapter – 15
    A New Path Begins 80

Chapter – 16
    Embracing New Horizons 88

Chapter – 17
    Shadows of the Past 96

Chapter – 18
    Elena's Journey Through the Pandemic Storm 102

Chapter – 19
    Shadows of Doubt 108

Chapter – 20
    Fragile Trust 115

Chapter – 21
    A Day of Rediscovery 120

Chapter – 22
    Veils of Silence and Shadows of Doubt 128

Chapter – 23
    Bridges and Brews: Exploring Bonds and Boundaries 132

Chapter – 24
    Peter's Aloofness and Mike's Friendship 136

Chapter – 25
    Elena's Journey Through Hope and Heartbreak 140

Chapter – 26
    Finding Peace and Purpose with Friends 145

Chapter – 27
    Digital Heartstrings: Elena's Quest for Connection 149

Chapter – 28
    Elena's Realization and Retreat 156

Chapter – 29
    Beyond University Walls: Journeys of Friendship and Futures 163

Chapter – 30
    Abroad Beginnings: From Homeland to Hamburg, Germany 170

Chapter – 31
    New Land, New Friends: Unveiling Paths 175

Chapter – 32
    Journeys of Elena DeSanta: A Tale of Dreams and Destinies 182

Chapter - 0
Roots and Crossroads

In the heart of Soweto, where the streets hummed with the rhythm of life, Elena DeSanta came into the world. Her presence signalled the start of a story intertwined with love, heritage, and the happy dance of fate.

Born into a Spanish family amidst the vibrant tapestry of South Africa, Elena's story began amid a convergence of cultures that painted the landscape of her existence. Her story, however, was not limited by ethnicity or custom. It was a tale of migration, the enduring embrace of love, and the intricate tapestry that fate stitched together.

Elena's family history began with her great-grandfather, a dreamer who left Santander, Spain to travel to the busy streets of Soweto in search of uncharted territory and unending possibilities. His transcontinental trip had planted the seeds of a history of resiliency, bravery, and the unwavering pursuit of aspirations that would last for many years.

However, Elena's tale was about more than simply genealogy and heritage; it was also about love, migration, and the coming together of destiny. Her parents exhibited the spirit of togetherness despite differences; they were models of cultural fusion and unending love.

The allure of friendship and the whispers of adventure drew her mother Carla, an adventurous Italian girl, to the coast of South Africa. She had no idea that her path would take her to the energetic metropolis of Cape Town, where she would have a fortuitous meeting that would permanently change the trajectory of her life. She met Elena's father Miguel amid the busy streets and vibrant hearts of Cape Town—a proud son of Spain whose origins are deeply ingrained yet smoothly woven into the cadence of African life. The fires of fate ignited a kinship between them that was as unexpected as it was durable, bridging linguistic and cultural divides.

Amidst the vivid colours of South Africa's varied landscapes, their union signalled the start of a new chapter filled with kid laughter, the warmth of times spent together, and the eternal search for identity and belonging.

A monument to the beauty of variety and the resiliency of the human spirit, Elena's early years were a symphony of languages, laughter, and shared experiences, situated between two worlds. She was fortunate to have an older sister who was smart beyond her years. Elena gained proficiency in both the global language of English, which served as a bridge to the world outside their door, and the poetic cadence of Spanish, which was spoken in low tones between her father and siblings, in this melting pot of cultures.

Elena's narrative unfolded against the backdrop of Soweto, a city rich in history, variety, and hope for the future, as she travelled through the formative years of her life. And she realized that her story was only getting started as she stood at the intersection of the past and present. She saw it as a path of self-discovery and a tapestry of experiences waiting to be weaved.

Welcome to the world of Elena DeSanta—a world where roots run deep, and hearts know no borders.

Chapter - 1
Foundations and Relations

Elena's early years unfolded within the modest row house nestled amidst the vibrant streets of Soweto. It stood as a bastion against the tumultuous world outside, a sanctuary where the echoes of family resonated through its cramped corridors, weaving a tapestry of memories that would shape Elena's life in profound ways.

The simple exterior of the house concealed the amazing chaos that existed all around it daily. The place was a flurry of activity, with youngsters laughing, siblings teasing, and seniors sharing their calm wisdom. Generations clashed and blended together in the dance of life, with each room containing a tale and every nook a memory.

Her sister, a steadfast companion and occasional challenger, shared the intimate confines of their room with Elena. Together, they traversed the labyrinth of sisterhood, navigating the peaks and valleys of their relationship amidst towers of books and forgotten treasures.

Their father, the youngest among four siblings, brought a youthful vigour to the household, infusing the air with his irrepressible energy and infectious enthusiasm. His presence was a beacon of light, illuminating even the darkest corners of their shared space with warmth and vitality.

Uncle Alejandro, with his easy smile and boundless laughter, added a touch of levity to the family dynamic. His tales of adventure and escapades beyond the city limits filled the air with a sense of wonder, transporting the family to distant lands and far-off worlds.

The family was made more competitive and friendly by Elena's relatives, a sister called Natalia and a brother named Alejandro Jr., also known as Junior. Their laughter echoed down the hallways as they played endless games of pretend and tag, their innocent joy bringing life to the otherwise dead silence. Their presence injected an extra layer of excitement into family gatherings, transforming mundane moments into cherished memories that would linger in the depths of Elena's mind for years to come.

And then there were Elena's grandparents, the steadfast pillars of wisdom and strength. Their quiet presence offered a sense of stability amidst the ever-changing landscape of family life, their gentle guidance shaping the values and traditions that bound the family together. Within the walls of their row house, Elena's childhood was a tapestry woven with threads of love, laughter, and shared experiences. It was a home filled with warmth and affection, where the bonds of family grew stronger with each passing day.

And so, amidst the hustle and bustle of everyday life, Elena's story began—a journey marked by the ordinary moments that shaped her into the person she would become. It was a life defined by the simple pleasures of family and friendship, where love was the guiding force that illuminated even the darkest of days.

As Elena reflected on her childhood memories, she couldn't help but acknowledge the stark contrast between her recollections and the reality she now faced. The row house, once a bustling hub of warmth and affection, seemed to have lost some of its luster in the passage of time. While it wasn't entirely the opposite of what she remembered, the dynamics within the family had shifted, and the atmosphere felt tinged with a sense of tension and uncertainty. Despite her longing for the comforting familiarity of the past, Elena realized that life was rarely as idyllic as childhood memories painted it to be.

Elena, Alejandro Jr., and Natalia, her cousins, were the architects of boundless adventures that danced through the corridors of their home. Together, they crafted worlds of imagination, where paper planes soared high and dreams knew no bounds. Their laughter, a symphony of innocence, echoed against the backdrop of familial discord, offering moments of respite amidst the brewing storm.

Between the adults, tensions simmered, a silent tempest veiled beneath the facade of civility. Elena's father and Alejandro, bound by the ties of friendship and shared history, exchanged gifts as tokens of enduring camaraderie—a silent testament to the warmth that flickered within the shadows.

In contrast, Elena's aunt, Carmen, held her children close, her watchful gaze a shield against the uncertainties that lurked beyond their doorstep. Though not unkind to Elena, her actions spoke volumes of the barriers that stood between them, casting a shadow over the tapestry of familial bonds.

Yet, amidst the turmoil, Elena found solace in the embrace of her grandmother—a beacon of love and wisdom amidst the chaos of everyday life. Together, they embarked on daily journeys to the bustling streets below, their footsteps a gentle cadence against the symphony of urban life.

Conversely, Elena's relationship with her grandfather was tinged with complexity—a dance of misunderstandings and missed connections. His half-deafness created a chasm between them, a silent divide that widened with each passing day.

As the days turned into weeks, tensions within the family reached a crescendo—a cacophony of whispered grievances and unspoken truths. It was a delicate balance, teetering on the edge of collapse, waiting for the slightest breath to push it over the precipice.

The sickness of Elena's mother, a spectre that loomed large over their formerly tranquil home, served as the impetus. A sense of desperation pervaded the room as Elena's father turned to Carmen. His entreaty for help was greeted with resistance, resulting in a power struggle that reverberated through the walls and broke the flimsy façade of familial harmony. After that, as the reverberations of their argument vanished into thin air, Elena's family found themselves in a precarious situation where hope for the future was tempered by fear.

Elena's family then set off on a trip into the unknown, one that was lighted by the promise of fresh starts and the fading embers of hope, among the turmoil and strife. It was a voyage that would influence the very fabric of their lives for years to come, and it was a monument to the human spirit's tenacity and the eternal power of love in the face of hardship.

In the middle of the turmoil and disputes, Elena learned important truths that spoke to the core of her being. She discovered that the path of life is a tapestry made of threads representing both happiness and sadness, and that times of victory are sometimes preceded by hardships. During the chaos, she learned that resiliency is created in the furnace of difficulties and that the real test of a person's strength is their capacity to withstand the storms life throws at the human soul. Elena discovered wisdom in the echoes of family strife, realizing that change and rebirth are possible even in the midst of darkness.

As the sun dipped low on the horizon, casting golden hues upon the canvas of Elena's young life, her family embarked on a transformative journey, leaving behind the familiar comforts of their former abode for the promise of a one-bedroom apartment—a modest haven that would serve as the crucible for their collective dreams and aspirations.

Within the confines of their humble dwelling, the echoes of determination reverberated, woven into the very fabric of their existence by the steadfast resolve of Elena's father. From the depths of adversity, he emerged as a paragon of resilience, his brow furrowed with the sweat of labour, his hands calloused by the toil of countless hours spent toiling in pursuit of a better tomorrow. With each dawn, he rose with unwavering purpose, a testament to the enduring power of perseverance and the boundless depths of parental love.

Amidst the walls of their newfound sanctuary, familial bonds flourished, unfurling like petals of a blossoming flower in the gentle embrace of affection. Each weekend brought the arrival of Elena's grandmother, a beacon of warmth and joy whose radiant smile illuminated the dim corridors of their humble abode. With arms outstretched and heart aglow, she bestowed upon Elena treasures of love and wisdom, each gift a testament to the enduring legacy of familial devotion.

In the bustling streets of their burgeoning neighbourhood, Elena's world expanded, unfurling like the pages of an unwritten story waiting to be told. With the school nestled within arm's reach, she embarked on a journey of discovery and enlightenment, her footsteps a cadence of youthful exuberance and boundless curiosity.

Within the hallowed halls of academia, Elena found solace in the friendship of Isabella—a kindred spirit whose laughter echoed through the corridors of childhood, a beacon of companionship amidst the ebb and flow of youthful camaraderie. Together, they forged a bond as enduring as the sands of time, their laughter a melody that danced upon the winds of destiny.

Yet, amidst the tapestry of childhood joys, shadows loomed on the horizon, casting a pall over the sun-kissed landscape of innocence. Bullies, with hearts veiled in darkness, prowled the corridors of youth, their taunts a discordant symphony that pierced the tender fabric of Elena's soul. Tears stained her cheeks as she weathered the storm of rejection, her tender heart aching with each unkind word.

Through the tempest of adversity, Elena found refuge in the tender embrace of her mother—a bastion of strength and compassion amidst the tumult of adolescence. In her mother's arms, she discovered the true essence of unconditional love—a force that transcended the trials of childhood, and illuminated the path towards self-discovery and resilience.

In the crucible of her solitary childhood, Elena forged bonds of steel—a testament to the resilience of the human spirit and the enduring power of love. And though her journey was fraught with challenges and tribulations, she emerged unbroken, a beacon of hope amidst the tumultuous seas of life's unfolding saga, her spirit unyielding, her heart aflame with the promise of a brighter tomorrow.

Deep lessons were woven throughout Elena's life, amid the interplay of happiness and sadness, success and failure. She discovered the subtle differences between loyalty and trust via the company of real friends and the hurt of betrayal. She learned to weather life's storms with steadfast resolution from adversity, which was a crucible for growth and shaped her resilience. Love, dazzling and complex, became her beacon of light, giving her confidence and compassion with every stride. Elena welcomed the unknown with a hopeful heart as she stood on the precipice of the unknown, prepared to go on into the unexplored regions of the future.

In the heart of their humble abode, nestled amidst the vibrant streets of Soweto, Elena's world expanded with each passing day. She set off on a voyage of wonder and discovery at the tender age of four, and her days were filled with the endless enthusiasm of juvenile discovery.

Elena discovered her family's loving embrace to be the foundation upon which her travels would be built. Her parents, Miguel and Carla, provided her with kind care and encouragement to pursue her endless curiosity, fostering an atmosphere where joy and discovery were possible at every turn. Together, they created a tapestry of laughter and love that was unbounded by Elena's imagination.

Within the magical domain of their living room, Elena's most treasured toys evolved into loyal allies through imaginative adventures and audacious dares. She set off on incredible adventures that took her to far-off places and magical worlds while holding a doll in one hand and a tiny car in the other. Like her father, Elena loved cars and was enthralled with the world of motors despite the toys her parents had purchased her. The sound of engines and the rush of speed ignited her imagination.

Sofia, Elena's older sister, accompanied her in the fun, her protective demeanour and gentle direction influencing Elena's early life. Elena found solace in Sofia's warmth and insight as they explored the joys of childhood together.

The world waited outside their door, full of exciting discoveries and fresh experiences. The laughing of Elena's little friends found her in the busy streets of their neighbourhood; their light-hearted banter was a tribute to the happiness that comes with youthful companionship.

Elena spent her days in their garden, among the tall trees and golden sunshine, enjoying the small pleasures of discovery. She danced among the glories of nature, chasing butterflies across fields of wildflowers, her laughter blending with the soft air. Elena found the ageless wisdom of experience and the unbreakable force of familial ties in the warm embrace of her grandparents. Their tales captured the essence of bygone eras with vivid descriptions, captivating her imagination with tales of far-off places and fantastical animals.

Elena's heart grew full of appreciation for the beauty all around her as the sun sank low in the horizon, providing a warm warmth. The greatest gift of all was found in her family's embrace: an unfathomable love and a sense of belonging that would accompany her throughout her life.

Thus began the narrative of Elena, amid the laughter and delight of infancy; it is a monument to the eternal power of love and the limitless glories of youth. Elena was only starting her travels in the centre of Soweto, where hopes and possibilities were many and dreams took to the skies.

Chapter - 2
Embracing the Majesty of Drakensberg

On a radiant morning filled with promise, Elena's heart danced with excitement as she penned a request for a week's respite from the corridors of academia. Elena's eyes gleamed with excitement as she broke the exciting news that she and her parents were visiting Drakensberg when her school teacher asked about the leave. She was filled with excitement as she got ready to travel to Drakensberg, a place that drew explorers and dreamers alike with its unmatched beauty and untamed wilderness.

Drakensberg, dear reader, is not merely a destination; it is a realm of breath taking vistas and untold wonders, nestled in the heart of South Africa like a jewel waiting to be discovered. Its rugged peaks, shrouded in mist and legend, tower over rolling hills and verdant valleys, inviting all who dare to explore its hidden treasures.

Picture yourself, if you will, the towering cliffs, their old faces worn by weather and time, rising stubbornly against an unending expanse of sky. Rivers that meander over the countryside below reveal secrets to the wind via their sparkling waters. The land is painted in shades of scarlet, gold, and blue by fields of wildflowers that cover the valleys; the resulting tapestry of colour matches that of the most vivid dreams.

For Elena and her family, the trip to the Drakensberg was an opportunity to connect with the fundamental forces that built the globe and a pilgrimage to the very centre of nature rather than simply a simple holiday. It was a chance to get away from the rush of contemporary life and reacquaint yourself with the earth's rhythms.

The road in front of them seemed like a ribbon of promise as they embarked on their journey, snaking through charming towns and expansive views. With every bend and curve, a new vista opened up, and every peak provided a different viewpoint on the wonders that awaited.

Elena's pulse raced with excitement when they finally arrived and saw the breathtaking magnificence of Drakensberg. She felt a connection to something bigger than herself here, amidst the soaring peaks and tumbling waterfalls.

Together with her family, Elena ventured into the heart of this untamed wilderness, her senses alive with the sights, sounds, and scents of nature in all its glory. They hiked along winding trails that led to hidden valleys and secluded waterfalls, their laughter mingling with the song of birds and the rustle of leaves.

Striding up steep cliffs and jagged ledges to get the ideal viewpoint, they reached breathtaking altitudes. And when they finally arrived at the top, their efforts were repaid tenfold by the sight of an incredibly beautiful vista that spanned the planet.

In the nights, people gathered around blazing campfires, laughing and telling stories under a canopy of glittering lights, as the sun sank below the horizon and the stars came out to dance in the velvet sky. They discovered a sense of harmony and serenity in the embrace of the nature here; their connection went beyond words to speak to the core of their beings.

Elena had a twinge of melancholy as their stay in Drakensberg came to an end since she would be leaving this magical place behind. She was aware, however, that the memories they had created would be with her always— a monument to the strength of familial ties and the enduring force of nature.

Dear reader, As Elena's trip to the Drakensberg comes to an end, dear reader, let us celebrate the wonders of this unique location—a place where dreams come true and adventure has no bounds. A world of wonder lies inside the embrace of the Drakensberg, between its majestic peaks and infinite horizons, urging us to discover its hidden gems and revel in its breathtaking beauty. So, let's enjoy the beauty of this magnificent terrain, where each peak and valley offers the possibility of exploration and each sunset transforms the sky into a magical place. Let's embrace Drakensberg's charm and celebrate the limitless opportunities that lie just beyond the horizon together.

As the sun set on the tranquil landscapes of Drakensberg, casting a golden glow upon the rolling hills and verdant valleys, Elena's heart was heavy with the weight of tragedy. It was a day etched in sorrow, a poignant reminder of life's fragility and the inevitability of loss.

After returning from their trip through the beauty of nature, Elena was devastated to learn of her grandfather's loss. His abrupt and untimely death upended their family's world of peace. They set out on a voyage of sadness, their hearts heavy and their eyes streaked with tears as they struggled with the hard reality of their beloved patriarch's departure.

At the age of five, Elena found herself on the verge of despair as her little heart found it difficult to accept that death was inevitable. She stayed calm, her feelings hidden behind a curtain of doubt, while others sobbed freely. Maybe it was her youthful purity that saved her from feeling the full force of grief, or maybe it was her ignorance that prevented her from crying. Still, her little size obscured the extent of her loss, a mute monument to the tremendous influence of death on the human spirit.

Her cousin and confidante, Natalia, took the brunt of the loss; her tears were a flood of unfiltered passion that threatened to overwhelm her frail soul. She cried uncontrollably, her sadness a haunting symphony that reverberated through the halls of their shared sorrow, unable to contain her misery. It was evidence of their strong relationship, which had been strengthened by love and forged in the furnace of family.

Grandmother Rosa, who was sitting on the ground amid the solemn assembly, was crying uncontrollably since her husband had passed away. Her sobs reverberated through the atmosphere, a lament for the years they had spent together and the experiences they had created. Her tears were an expression of the profound sadness she was feeling and the unwavering love that united them.

The circumstances surrounding her grandfather's death only contributed to the already heavy sadness that enveloped their home. He was eighty years old, having lived a long and meaningful life, and his presence had been a source of strength and knowledge for them. His premature death after a fall from his bed was a sobering reminder of the erratic character of life and its transient nature.

Elena experienced a hard awakening to the terrible facts of mortality, which was a depressing realization. The days of innocent youth were gone, to be replaced by the grim realities of life and death. She was obliged to face the harsh reality of her own mortality, a concept that persisted in the back of her mind. She could no longer cling to the consoling idea of immortality.

Elena had a greater respect for the wonderful gift of life as they put her grandfather to rest in a sombre ceremony filled with tears and hushed prayers. During the quiet minutes of contemplation that ensued, she made a commitment to treasure every moment that was passing, to appreciate the beauty of the present, and to pay tribute to the memories of those who had come before her.

Elena found the unchangeable truth that death is not the end but rather a new beginning—a voyage into the unknown led by the undying light of love and the promise of eternal peace—in the fabric of life, stitched with threads of pleasure and pain, love and loss.

Elena's trip so continued until sunset, leaving behind its last rays of light on the planet, serving as a monument to the human spirit's resiliency and the eternal strength of love in the face of hardship. For it was in the furnace of loss that she found the unbounded resources of her own power and the transforming force of grief—a voyage that would profoundly influence the trajectory of her life for years to come.

Elena accepted the lessons of the past as she stood on the precipice of a fresh start, finding courage and resolve in the recollections of her cherished grandfather. After all, the lasting legacy of love that lighted her path and helped her go forward, one step at a time, was what ultimately defined her, not the anguish of loss.

Dear reader, let us cling to the knowledge that we are never really alone, even in the depths of our darkest moments. Let us find comfort in the unshakable presence of love and the eternal links of family that lead us home as we say farewell to the shadows of loss and welcome the dawn of a new day. We take comfort in the understanding that love and connection weave an eternal road towards healing and rebirth, even in the midst of the complex tapestry of life's pleasures and sufferings, victories and trials. May the bright light of love give us courage as it illuminates our path now and forevermore, bringing us closer and closer to the cosy embrace of home.

Chapter - 3
Embracing Family and Community

In the intricate tapestry of Elena's life, the bonds with her cousins were threads woven with laughter, mischief, and a shared sense of belonging. Their reciprocal get-togethers and trips to Elena's home served as the cornerstone of their familial bond, assembling a colourful tapestry of common experiences that cut across time and space.

Every Sunday, the DeSanta family made a sombre trek to the church located next to Tío Alejandro's modest home; this holy ritual gave them comfort and reverence. Seeing how much Elena missed her dear cousins, she would frequently beg her father to leave her off at Tío Alejandro's house on Saturdays so she could look forward to her happy reunion with her family the next day.

Every week, Rosa, Elena's grandma, who was a constant in their life, would make the trip from Tío Alejandro's home to Elena's family to show them her affection and warmth. The sound of generations past reverberated in her embrace, demonstrating the lasting power of familial ties that endured over time.

Across the bustling street from Tío Alejandro's dwelling stood another pillar of resilience and fortitude—Tía Maria, Elena's father's sister. Elena's father was his sister. Elena was just a baby when Tía Maria's husband passed away, leaving her to gracefully and resolutely negotiate the turbulent seas of single parenting.

Isadora and Mateo were Tía Maria's two children, and she gave them her whole attention and care. Isadora was a lively person with a mischievous sparkle in her eyes. She had a unique affinity with Elena, and their laughter reverberated throughout the neighbourhood as they went on several excursions together. Elena's junior by a year, Mateo instilled in their home a spirit of carefree abandon, his contagious laughter resonating through the hallways of their common life.

Elena found inspiration and hope in Tía Maria's perseverance in the face of hardship, which is a monument to the enduring power of love and sacrifice. Elena gained an understanding of the value of tenacity and resolve in the face of adversity from Tía Maria. Elena lived with Tía Maria and saw firsthand the extreme injustice and suffering that characterized their neighbourhood.

The contrast between wealth and poverty made a lasting impression on Elena and gave her a strong desire to fight for equality and justice for everyone. Elena took with her the priceless lessons she had learnt from the ties of family and community as she made her way through life's maze. Her journey ahead was illuminated with bravery and resiliency by their love and support, which she used as a beacon.

Elena set off with the certainty that she would never be travelling alone. Formed by the infinite love of her family and the colourful mosaic of her community, she addressed the challenges and doubts that lay ahead with resolute determination. She found strength in the unity of spirit that united them, as well as a source of bravery and hope, in their embrace. Elena took comfort in the idea that no matter how difficult the path ahead may appear, she could traverse it with courage, grace, and the unshakable promise of a better tomorrow because of their shared experiences and steadfast support.

Tío Alejandro's house was a bustling hug, with cousins laughing and the wonderful song of childlike delight filling the air. Elena was sitting atop the worn fence with Junior, her always eager and mischievous partner, their young souls dancing in the warm embrace of family ties. The sun shone on their excursions, casting a golden light that filled the landscape with colours of limitless possibilities as they manoeuvred through the complicated dance of laughter and balance. Every second was a chance for exploration, every stride a confirmation of the unwavering spirit of youthful curiosity.

However, amid the symphony of happiness, fate unfurled its arbitrary hand and Elena was flung from her perch, the ground coming up to snatch her with frightening rapidity. With a dull thud, she collided with the earth, her forehead bearing the brunt of the fall, a silent witness to the fragility of human existence.

Elena's most hopeless moment was brightened by Tía Carmen's unflinching presence, who took on the role of her stalwart protector in the absence of her loving grandma. Cradling Elena with the warmth of a mother's love, she drew Elena into her arms with soft hands and a compassionate heart.

With the weight of Elena's suffering on their shoulders, they set out to visit the doctor together. The amount of tears Elena shed was evident, demonstrating the intensity of her pain, and Tía Carmen's comforting murmurs provided comfort in the face of uncertainty.

Elena's wound was carefully tendered to in the sterile examining room, the sting of the antiseptic serving as a cruel reminder of life's unpredictability.

The doctor's gentle hands stitched together the frail strands of Elena's broken spirit, weaving a tapestry of healing with each stroke.

Elena was engulfed in her cousins' loving hug as the afternoon sun started to slowly set, their expressions filled with pity and worry. In their naivety, they tried to alleviate Elena's misery by providing toys, candies, and trinkets in an attempt to make her feel better.

But in the middle of the rush of gifts, Elena realized something very important: the real solace didn't come from the stuff surrounding her, but rather from the limitless resources of human connection and compassion. She found courage and comfort in the gentle embrace of her relatives' affection, a ray of hope in the darkness of misfortune.

Elena learned an important lesson in the midst of suffering and uncertainty: resilience is a symbol of the lasting strength of the human spirit rather than just a measure of physical strength. She learned about the transformational power of compassion—a force that transcended time and space—in the furnace of hardship. She felt overwhelmed with appreciation for all the good things in her life, including her family's affection, the warmth of friends, and the enduring strength of the human spirit, as the stars came out of their heavenly hiding places and shone down on the earth below.

Elena found a fundamental truth in the face of extreme hardship: hope is a resilient light that shines brightly on the way to recovery, atonement, and the unwavering promise of a better tomorrow, even in the darkest of situations. This deep insight is woven throughout the complex web of life's setbacks and victories, serving as a reminder of the human spirit's tenacity and ability to overcome hardship. When faced with difficulties, hope becomes the beacon of light that illuminates the path ahead and gives each moment the potential for regeneration and transformation. Elena accepted this sobering fact and took comfort in the idea that, despite all of life's complications, hope always triumphs and offers bravery, fortitude, and the promise of a new dawn.

Chapter - 4
The Tapestry of New Beginnings

As the days danced like shadows across the walls of their cramped one-bedroom apartment, Elena's family yearned for a breath of fresh air, a space to unfurl their dreams and aspirations. Her parents searched the maze of real estate ads for what seemed like an eternity, hoping to find a place where they could bury their hopes and feed their souls.

Their search was full of obstacles and requirements: they needed a ground-floor adobe or one with an elevator, which was made necessary by the ominous rumours about her grandfather's failing health. However, destiny, in its mysterious form, took an unanticipated turn when her grandfather, Juan, passed away, leaving a profound emptiness that echoed through their hearts.

A three-bedroom refuge tucked away in the heart of a friendly town rose above the waves of life's ups and downs. Elena's family set off on the journey to acquire their new adobe with trembling hands and bated breath, their spirits buoyed by the prospect of a better day.

As feelings were wrapped in tendrils of nostalgia and memories were crammed into cardboard boxes, the shift happened like a delicate ballet. Every object carried the weight of their common past, serving as a monument to the fabric of their shared experience.

A symphony of emotions, a mélange of exhilaration and apprehension interwoven like threads in a great tapestry, erupted within Elena's delicate heart at the possibility of a new home. The halls of the new flat pulsed with the boundless potential that waited like an unexplored treasure trove.

The familiar warmth of her family's hug gave Elena comfort in the middle of the mayhem, their laughter trailing through the atmosphere like delicate spiderweb threads. Each sound had the possibility of rebirth in its resonance, demonstrating the human spirit's ability to persevere in the face of hardship.

The purchase of their new house was more to her parents than just bricks and mortar; it was a testament to their everlasting will and perseverance.

Their house was a refuge of security and affection in an uncertain world, a monument to the resilience of the human spirit.

For her parents, owning a new house was more than just bricks and mortar; it represented their constant perseverance and will. Amidst an unpredictable environment, their house served as a stronghold of security and affection, demonstrating the resilience of the human being.

In the kaleidoscope of fresh beginnings, Elena's family embraced the dawn of a new chapter brimming with promise, opportunity, and the boundless horizons of the future. In moments of calm reflection, Elena saw that their trip was not just a physical one but also one of self-awareness, resiliency, and the never-ending search for a home, a place to belong, rather than a place to end up. Every step they took on their journey together was accompanied by the echoes of possibilities, leading them in the direction of the illusory beaches of fulfilment and belonging.

In the labyrinthine corridors of her school, Elena navigated a landscape fraught with the whispers of judgment and the echoes of laughter. Every day felt never-ending, a solitary voyage broken up by sporadic bursts of companionship and infrequent bursts of intimacy. But even among her classmates' busy crowd, Elena frequently felt lost and alone in a sea of faces.

Her young heart felt the burden of loneliness all the time, serving as a continuous reminder of the barriers that kept her and her classmates apart—barriers that she didn't want to reveal. Upon introspection, Elena found herself wondering: What was it in her that appeared to resist welcome and warmth? Was there a secret fault that she was unable to recognize, something that made her fundamentally flawed?

She developed the habit of turning to her mother for comfort and understanding during her turbulent school years. She would inquire, her voice shaking with vulnerability, "Mom, what's wrong with me?" Even still, Elena was unable to get rid of the sense of inadequacy that was eating away at her spirit, despite her mother's kind consolation and words of comfort.

She sought solace in her home's safety despite the difficulties she had at school. She could take off the mask of loneliness that was weighing her down there among the comforting familiarity and family, and bask in the affection that was given to her without conditions, like a warm hug.

Elena found solace and brightness in Isabella, her dependable friend through the turbulent waters of youth, who stood by her side throughout her lonely moments. A lifeline in a world that sometimes felt cold and cruel, their connection was forged in the furnace of shared experiences and understanding. Their relationship grew closer every day as they navigated the ups and downs of puberty together.

Nonetheless, Elena experienced loneliness like a persistent spectre that tormented her every waking hour, even in her own house. The previously unshakable tie she had with her older sister, Sofia, started to crumble at the edges as time and the upheaval of puberty tugged at their relationship.

Elena longed for the intimacy they previously enjoyed, for the times when pleasure and laughter filled the air like the lovely aroma of springtime blooms, desperately trying to overcome the widening gap between them. However, despite her greatest attempts, Elena felt as though there was a growing gap between them every day, leaving her adrift in an ocean of doubt.

Elena looked to her mother for direction and comfort as she attempted to fill the space left by Sofia's declining presence. She confessed, her voice full of a tangible feeling of desire, "Mom, I need someone else to play with." Her mother said, "Pray to God, my dear, and He will surely listen," and although her words were brief, they contained a powerful truth.

Thereby, on every Sunday, Elena would bow her head in silent adoration inside the church's sacred halls, her little fists clenched in prayer as she uttered her sincere requests to the sky above. During those rare times of introspection, she ventured to believe that the warmth of sibling connections that would endure a lifetime would soon replace the loneliness of her school days.

One day, though, her mother surprised her by telling her that a baby was developing within her. At the age of six, Elena found it difficult to process the news that her mother was pregnant since her developing mind was not yet mature enough to fully process it. The prospect of a new existence and a new sibling to share her pleasures and sufferings, victories and tribulations, nonetheless, kindled a glimmer of hope inside her despite the confusion and uncertainty.

As she set off on this voyage of wonder and expectation, Elena held onto the faint hope that maybe, in this new phase of her life, she might discover the friendship and connection she so much needed. In her lonely times of contemplation, she ventured to hope that the cold shadow of her school days would soon give way to the warmth of sibling connections, forged through shared experiences and unflinching support. Elena's heart glowed with the hope of creating bonds that would last and brighten her path with the everlasting light of kinship as she waded through the unexplored seas of anticipation.

In the gentle ebb and flow of time, as the days melded into weeks and the sun painted the sky with hues of amber and gold, Elena's home hummed with the palpable anticipation of new life. A symphony of hope and expectancy began to slowly fill her mother's abdomen, and with each passing instant, the marvel of creation unfolding inside her was confirmed.

While enduring the agony of pregnancy, Elena's mother shows both fortitude and affection. She exuded an unshakable dedication to her family despite the weariness and suffering that frequently accompanied her illness. Even though she was tired, her hands kept working softly and carefully, cooking, taking care of housework, and loving her kids unconditionally.

Elena, always the whirlwind of a child's enthusiasm, was caught up in the wave of excitement that blew through their house like a soft wind. Her heart ached for a sibling to come along so they might enjoy childhood adventures and the delights of sibling bonding. She prayed more fervently for a sibling every day, whispering her wishes to close friends and family and to herself in her silent chamber.

But behind all of the excitement bubbling up inside of Elena, there was a sacred trust at work—a secret that needed to be kept safe. Her lips were shut against the want to let the world in on her excitement as she carried the weight of her mother's pregnancy with significant reverence. Elena knew the value of her mother's confidence and guarded it like a priceless gem, despite her heart's desire to confide in companions.

Elena would sneak out with Isabella or an older friend at uncontrollably excited moments, her joy showing through in whispered confidentialities and laughs. Together, they exulted in the prospect of fresh life, the promise of the unknown dancing in their hearts.

With weeks instead of days, Elena's excitement surged like a wave, her pulse racing at the thought of fresh starts and endless opportunities. She was counting down the days before her family would receive their newest addition, and as time went on, her prayers blended with the soft rhythms of daily life.

Elena felt more and more excited every day as she waited for the baby to arrive, the air filled with whispers of expectation and a soft hum of enthusiasm. The bright colours of optimism and joy that surrounded her early existence were enhanced by the approaching birth of her sibling, which shone brightly on the road ahead. The infant ignited her imagination with fantasies of romance and adventure that remained unrealized, a beacon of promise in the vibrant mosaic of her life.

The anticipation in Elena's heart reached a fever pitch as she noticed her father waiting to pick her up from school, a departure from their usual routine. As they set out on an unexpected expedition, the reason for which was still a mystery, her mind was racing with questions. When she arrived at the hospital, the seriousness of the situation started to set in, and her father's silence only served to heighten her sense of mystery. The atmosphere hung thick with the weight of imminent change, and the air crackled with every instant that passed.

Elena's mother Carla left a path of anxious excitement in her wake as the hours passed and she was swept away into the quiet hospital halls. The world held its breath, anticipating a historic moment, in the stillness of the night.

Elena saw the miracle of birth play out in front of her eyes in the silence of the hospital room, her mother's bravery and tenacity serving as a ray of hope in the uncertainty. The pace of life intensified with each passing minute, and fresh starts were always in the air.

The universe then welcomed a new soul into its midst amid murmured prayers and frightened hearts amid the silence of the night—a priceless gift enveloped in the gentle embrace of destiny. A newborn's cry reverberated throughout the space, a symphony of life that infused the air with the delightful sound of opportunity.

Elena's heart was so full of thankfulness and excitement when she saw her newborn brother for the first time. With his birth, a new chapter in their family's history was opened, demonstrating the eternal strength of love and the limitless possibilities of hope. With her heart bursting with an unfathomable warmth from July's embrace, Elena looked down at her infant brother and felt his tiny fingers clinging to life with a purity that spoke to her soul.

Elena could not help but smile as she thought of the reunion that would greet her and her father and sister when they got back home. There was a feast of love and laughter waiting for them when they returned, and her cherished grandma waited at the entrance, her arms wide in welcome.

A beacon of light in the fabric of their lives, Elena's baby brother's presence would one day bring them together at home, and her heart would dance with anticipation. She accepted the teachings that came with his presence with every passing second, the subtle reminder of the wonders that were concealed in the ordinary. Thus, with wide arms and a heart full of love, Elena welcomed her newborn brother Diego into the world as the stars twinkled overhead and the night murmured its secrets. Diego's name is a monument to the everlasting beauty of their common history.

With her little brother born, Elena realized that their family had embarked upon a wonderful adventure with countless opportunities as they adapted to their new duties as a family of five. They so welcomed the start of a new chapter in their life, bonded by the unshakable bonds of family and united in love. Their hearts were filled with joy and optimism. As time went on, they would travel the meandering paths of life side by side, their hearts entwined in a web of love and common experiences, as they set off on a path filled with laughter, endless happiness, and discover.

The DeSanta family was ecstatic to have Diego home, and his homecoming warmed and delighted them. Family members came from all around, their laughter resonating through the hallways and the aroma of festivity filling the air like a soft wind. Rosy, Elena's grandmother and the family matriarch was a beam of pride and joy, her wrinkled hands busy making sure everyone was fed and comfortable.

The next day dawned with the prospect of friendship and companionship, as Elena arrived at Isabella's home and felt at ease in her familiar surroundings. The urgent sound of the phone cut through the silence like a sharp knife, shattering the calm of the moment. When Isabella's mother heard the news that would change Elena's life forever, her voice quivered with emotion.

Isabella's mother responded, "Elena, pack your bags," her voice heavy with sorrow and incredulity.

When Elena's father, Miguel, showed up to pick her up along with her brothers and cousins, confusion raced through Elena's head. Their worried expressions revealed how serious the situation was, shrouding the once-jovial environment in the gloom. In the midst of doubt, one of her cousins broke the heartbreaking news that their cherished grandma, Rosy, had passed away.

The news rocked Elena's life, yet the love she had for Rosy remained unwavering. Rosy had been rushing around serving their visitors' lunch just the day before, her laughter filling the room. She had been the same this morning, smiling as she greeted guests from the balcony. But this afternoon, she vanished into an unending sleep, creating a gap that looked insurmountable.

Elena's cheeks were wet with tears as she struggled to accept her grandmother's death. The idea of Rosy being buried made them feel unimaginably sad, as her disappearance left a permanent hole in their lives. A sorrowful farewell was spoken to a beloved matriarch whose warmth and affection had been a ray of hope during their darkest hours.

Elena clung to the warmth of Rosy's embrace and the echo of her laughter in the days that followed, finding comfort in the memories they shared. Despite Rosy's passing, her memory endured in the hearts of her loved ones, serving as a beacon of hope while they processed their loss and dealt with their grief.

As they gathered to say their last goodbyes to Rosy, Elena vowed fervently to honour her grandmother's memory by living each day with the same elegance, tenacity, and steadfast love that had characterized Rosy's life. Even though the loss of Rosy cast a shadow over their hearts, Elena took comfort in the knowledge that her spirit would live on in their shared memories for eternity, serving as a reminder of the enduring power of love and family to support them through life's ups and downs.

Chapter - 5
Echoes of Discord

A year after the tragic death of their cherished matriarch, Rosy, the DeSanta family stood on the brink of uncertainty as the sun rose and set, symbolizing the passage of time. Diego, the hope of fresh starts, celebrated his first birthday amid their group's anguish, his laughter a salve to their broken hearts.

Miguel, the steadfast patriarch, toyed with the notion of a family vacation among the twinkling candles and exuberant laughter of Diego's birthday party. It would be an opportunity to add new experiences to the fabric of their lives and rekindle the ties that bind them. However, Miguel's ever-vigilant wife Carla wavered, her doubts putting a pall over his preparations like clouds blocking the light.

Elena, her young mind struggling with the intricacies of familial dynamics, found herself dragged into their discussions as their uneasiness rose and fell. Feeling the weight of their hesitation, she made a hesitant recommendation: how about consulting Sofia? After all, she would soon reach adulthood, and her insight and knowledge would be crucial in determining the way forward.

But Sofia, who was about to become an adult, didn't seem to be interested in their suggested excursion. Her apathy quickly gave way to disobedience, her words echoing like a clarion cry to break free from the bonds of familial relationships. There was an obvious sense of tension in the room, as the air was thick with worries and whispered realities.

Even though they tried to talk sense into Sofia's obstinate head, her unwillingness to travel with them served as a sharp reminder of the growing distance that had formed between parent and kid. After having a sad epiphany, Miguel and Carla decided to part ways with Sofia, her actions serving as a heartbreaking reminder of how brittle family ties can be.

Elena found herself struggling with a storm of contradictory feelings as the dust cleared and the memory of their dispute vanished into thin air.

These emotions included grief, disappointment, and a deep sense of loss. The thought of setting out on their adventure without Sofia loomed big, casting a cloud over the happiness that ought to have infused their preparations.

But even in the middle of the chaos, the DeSanta family's tenacity and hope for the future continued to shine brightly. Elena promised to treasure every moment as a reminder of the unbreakable strength of their familial relationship and to cling tightly to the memories they would make as they prepared for the adventure that lay ahead.

Elena stood at the start of a new chapter, emotions sorrowful but determined and resolute. The voyage that lay ahead of her was full of unknowns and challenges, but it also held the promise of adventure and renewal. She accepted the obstacles that were ahead as she set out on their journey together, strengthened by their familial ties and propelled by the fading optimism that glowed brightly inside each of them. They were united despite the uncertainties, prepared to face the twisting roads ahead with bravery, resiliency, and unyielding resolve.

The choice to travel to Kruger National Park was carefully considered after arguments and heated disputes within the family. The choice was fraught with ambiguity, as each family member considered their own preferences and concerns. Still, in the middle of the chaos, there was an unvoiced need for adventure, a desire to find comfort and companionship in the wild.

Miguel, Elena's father, had been the inspiration behind the concept, his eyes bright with the prospect of travel and learning. For him, the vastness of Kruger offered a chance to reestablish connections with the natural world and with one another, to create friendships that went beyond the little frustrations of daily existence. Elena's mother of Elena, Carla, had been less certain, her worries stemming from the practicality of travelling and her family's security. Though a part of her wished to watch her children's faces light up with awe amid the wild, her heart ached for the peace of home.

Trapped between her own want for adventure and the security of familiarity, Elena felt caught in the crossfire of her parents' conflicting feelings. She was filled with a tremendous sense of exhilaration that would not go away at the thought of discovering Kruger's wild beauty. The excitement of coming across lions and elephants, and seeing the unadulterated might of nature in action, filled her imagination.

Elena's older sister Sofia had opposed the plan the most. The concept of trekking through the forest with her family did not provide her with much comfort, as her thoughts were consumed with the intricacies of adulthood. The trivialities of adulthood and the quest for individuality and independence dominated her thoughts. She saw Kruger only as a transient diversion from her turbulent path of self-discovery.

And so, in the thick of family strife, a choice had to be made. His vision of adventure and togetherness is gaining out. With the hope of renewed relationships and shared experiences, the family would set off on a trek into the heart of Kruger National Park. Although Sofia had no desire to participate, she ultimately chose to do so.

Uncertainty hung in the air like morning mist as they embarked on their quest. But behind the surface remained a flicker of optimism, a conviction that deep moments of profound beauty and peacefulness might be discovered in the middle of life's turbulence. They would discover comfort, camaraderie, and the real meaning of family in the Kruger National Park, among the roar of lions and the trumpeting of elephants.

Elena's family set off on a tour into the heart of Kruger National Park in the gentle glow of morning, where the age-old rhythms of nature merged with their own heartbeats. Every family member was excited to discover the wonders that lay ahead of them in the vast wilderness, and they each brought a special combination of curiosity, enthusiasm, and expectation with them.

The cool morning air whispered stories of excitement and the possibility of amazing experiences as they clambered into the open-sided safari vehicle. Miguel's heart was overflowing with eagerness for the adventures that awaited, and his eyes glistened with delight. Carla's grin was a source of warmth and confidence in the face of uncertainty. Sofia's spirit yearned to be enveloped in the eternal embrace of the wild, as her gaze beamed with peaceful respect. With their eyes wide with amazement, Elena and Diego welcomed the adventure and prepared to fully enjoy their African safari.

They headed off into the vastness of the savannah with their seasoned ranger, Mandla, at the wheel, each turn of the wheel taking them closer to the centre of the wildness. The tall acacia trees reached up to the sky, with giraffe silhouettes hanging from their branches. The silhouettes looked calm and elegant against the early sun. A dazzling array of zebras, their black and white stripes glittering in the soft light, sprinted over the golden plains in perfect harmony.

A sense of majesty and wonder pervaded the air as a pride of lions basking in the warm warmth of the morning. Sofia's heart was moved by the untainted beauty of the wild, causing her breath to catch in her throat

as she saw their majestic presence. With a shared sense of astonishment, Miguel and Carla exchanged knowing glances that buoyed their spirits. With their youthful imaginations brimming with visions of exploration and adventure, Elena and Diego, cuddled up close, gasped at what they saw.

Amid the savannah's many delights, they stopped under the tall marula tree's shadow, its branches like an old friend's reaching out to comfort and protect from the scorching African heat. Nestled around an improvised table, covered with an abundance of fresh fruits and delicious sweets, they laughed and told stories, their voices harmonizing with the surrounding music of nature.

The warm warmth of a roaring campfire and the enticing smells of a traditional African feast greeted them back to camp as nightfall settled over the landscape, spreading shadows across the plains. With their faces softly lit by the fire, they gathered around the flickering flames beneath the huge expanse of the starry sky.

Miguel, Sofia, Elena, Diego, and Carla traded stories about their activities that day, their words creating an exquisite weaving of common experiences and treasured memories. A monument to the eternal link of family and the indomitable spirit of the human heart, the night air was filled with the sound of laughing and camaraderie at every turn.

Their hearts brimmed with appreciation for the wonder and beauty all about them as they took up residence in their tents under the watchful eye of the African night. As they journeyed together through the wild splendour of Kruger National Park, they discovered not just adventure and excitement but also a deep sense of serenity and belonging in the embrace of nature.

Elena was engulfed in a deep sense of comprehension as the African sunset and the night sky glistened with a million stars. In the majesty of the natural world, she had found the real meaning of family: the indestructible ties that connected their hearts together, the timeless memories that would carry them through life's journey, and the limitless love that outlasted every experience and hardship they shared.

Elena had discovered in the wide-open spaces of Kruger National Park that family was not limited to biological kin; rather, it was a fabric knit by common experiences, teasing, and the small moments of bonding that gave each day purpose. She had seen the love of her parents, the quiet tenacity of her sister, and the childlike wonder in her infant brother's eyes—all essential strands in the mosaic of their familial relationship.

Elena learned that true riches were found in the richness of connections formed in the furnace of life's experiences rather than in worldly belongings during the ups and downs of their safari journey. She silently vowed to treasure every second she spent with her family, to preserve the priceless memories they had built, and to cling to the love that united them for all eternity in the stillness of the African night.

A cocoon of newfound harmony surrounded Elena's family in the soft aftermath of their incredible journey across the wild reaches of Kruger National Park. The ties that had previously quarrelled under the strain of disagreement were now solid and unwavering, forged in the fire of common experiences and whispered secrets in the middle of nowhere.

After being an elusive nomad in their family's terrain, Sofia came back to the fold with a fresh drive and purpose. Her laughter had faded into the distance, but now it reverberated through their house, woven into the fabric of their everyday existence like a symphony that had been long forgotten yet joyfully discoverable.

Days after days, Sofia's path twisted towards the edge of possibility, where hopes reached the stars and dreams fluttered in the wind. She walked the meandering halls of academia with steadfast determination, her sights fixed on the far-off beaches of Stellenbosch University, a ray of hope hidden amid the stunning scenery of the Western Cape region.

Elena's family awaited Sofia's announcement of her success with bated breath; she had been accepted into Stellenbosch University, a recognition of her unshakable commitment and ceaseless quest for perfection. Their hearts swelled with pride at realizing her limitless potential, and the air crackled with excitement as they hailed her success.

But somewhere at the back of Elena's mind, amid the cheers, there was a tone of melancholy. A shadow of her adored sister's imminent departure hung over the festivities, serving as a poignant reminder of time's fleeting nature and change's unstoppable march.

While Sofia painstakingly organized her journey to Stellenbosch, Elena was tormented by a whirlwind of contradictory feelings, her soul whipped by the turbulent winds of hope and grief. She longed for more time spent with her sister, for times infused with the comforting embrace of sibling friendship and the warmth of shared laughter.

But even in the middle of the sadness of leaving, Elena found comfort in the quiet spaces of reflection. She came to see that, despite its frightening nature, change was an unavoidable part of life—a sign of fresh starts, a spur to development, and a monument to the human spirit's tenacity.

Elena learned a lot about accepting uncertainty and appreciating the beauty in life's fleeting fabric as Sofia was about to go. She found that the ties of family held firm, securing them to the shores of love and kinship, even in the midst of change.

Elena stood at the start of a new chapter, her heart a kaleidoscope of emotions, tinged with the sadness of farewells yet lighted by the brilliance of optimism, as Sofia set out for Stellenbosch. She discovered the strength to welcome change, embrace the unknown, and treasure the eternal ties that united them now and forever despite the distances and moments that separated them in the ever-changing currents of life.

Elena was struggling to understand the deep truths that life's changes taught her throughout the chaos of emotions that engulfed their house and Sofia's impending departure. As Sofia's voyage to Stellenbosch University came and went, Elena learned about the transforming power of change and the lasting strength of familial bonds.

Elena understood as she bid farewell to her sister that change was not just something to be dreaded but also a signpost for development and rejuvenation that showed the way to uncharted territory. When Sofia left, she took comfort in her family's unfailing devotion, which acted as a solid anchor during the storm of change.

Elena accepted the natural beauty of life's ups and downs via both humorous and tearful times, realizing that while saying goodbye may signal the end of one chapter, it also signals the start of a new one. She learned the true depth of the ties that held their family together while Sofia was away, creating a weaving of love and resiliency that was impervious to time and space.

Elena discovered, in short, that the unwavering strength of familial bonds stabilized the transformational force of change among life's currents, anchoring her heart to the shores of love and resilience, now and forever.

Chapter - 6
Unfamiliar Feelings

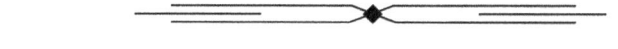

As the sun rose, a sense of excitement mixed with the anxious energy that hummed through the classroom hallways on the first day of school. As Sofia carefully packed her belongings and got ready for her departure to Stellenbosch University, it was the start of a new chapter in her life. Elena, on the other hand, was all fired up about going from third to fourth grade and was preparing herself emotionally for the change.

Curiosity and fascination rippled out from a fresh arrival amidst the sea of familiar faces. Elena was unaware of the boy who entered the classroom, and his presence unnerved her fragile heart. Her striking looks, so different from her own, elicited an unusual feeling of fluttering butterflies in her stomach or an alien pull tugging at the edges of her awareness.

Little and unsure, Elena was slowly approaching puberty when she became entangled in a web of strange feelings and struggled to make sense of experiences she could not believe. She felt as though the boy's easy charisma and appeal overshadowed her own identity, leaving her adrift in a sea of uncertainties and fears.

Beneath the veneer of youthful innocence, Elena harbored a secret burden—a gnawing sense of inadequacy, fueled by the taunts and jeers of her peers. Bullied for her perceived shortcomings, she bore the weight of their words like a heavy cloak, each barb piercing her fragile sense of self-worth.

As the days passed, Elena made her way through the maze of school life, her heart a battlefield of opposing feelings. Clad in the darkness of insecurity, she yearned to emerge into the open, to free herself from the chains of self-doubt and accept the entirety of her existence. But even in the face of uncertainty, she found comfort in her family's unshakable devotion, which acted as a ray of hope during the storm. As time went on, she found solace in their unwavering acceptance of her, their conviction in her intrinsic value resonating through the passageways of her spirit.

Elena made the decision to face her anxieties head-on with bravery and elegance, even if the road ahead appeared to be full of obstacles. Behind the surface of uncertainty, there was a heart full of unrealized potential and a spirit that aspired to fly above the boundaries of fear and doubt.

With unyielding conviction, Elena embraced the unknown and set off on a self-discovery adventure, led by the bright glow of her own inner light. Because deep down she understood that real beauty didn't come from external appearances but rather from the limitless depths of her own soul.

Through the complex web of teenage drama and school politics, Elena discovered that the most important fights weren't waged on the fields of external approval but rather in the sacred rooms of her own heart. And she embraced the difficult yet thrilling path of self-acceptance and self-love as she moved forward, her spirit burning with the fire of resolve.

Within the sacred corridors of school life, amid the rising and falling tide of foolishness, Elena was thrown headlong into the turbulent waters of adolescence, where ignorance and innocence clashed in a tempest of misinterpretation.

Elena's concentration wandered, lost in a sea of wonder and perplexity, as the teacher's voice sank into the background, engulfed by the cacophony of the classroom. The classroom burst into an eruption of noise during the teacher's brief departure, and the air was heavy with the overwhelming energy of youth.

Elena had no idea that a single phrase, its ramifications hidden under the mask of innocence, had been inscribed on the bench's surface and her reality. "Sexy," she said, the sounds unfamiliar to her tongue like a riddle she had to solve. She repeated the term carelessly, without understanding its meaning, and her voice resounded across the large classroom.

The teacher's outrage and disbelief were evident in her strong voice as she responded to her unexpected declaration. Elena emerged from the classroom in a fog of confusion, her innocence shattered by the sting of miscommunication, and she faced the hard realities of puberty.

The truth revealed itself to Elena in the privacy of the hallway, resembling a delicate flower with delicate petals that revealed secrets about the world outside. The teacher's answer illuminated the murky edges of ignorance by illuminating the actual significance of the term that she had unintentionally uttered. Elena was confused, her purity stained by the pain of shame and misinterpretation as she struggled with the hard realities of life. But in the middle of the uncertainty, a glimmer of hope sprang from inside her, a spark of resilience.

Miguel's smile wavered at the realisation of her lost innocence as she took comfort in her father's hug. He signed the incriminating statement with a heavy heart, his signature serving as a symbol of the unity that held them through their difficult times. However, Elena found comfort in the knowledge that embraced her gently in the midst of adolescence, her voyage of self-discovery unfolding among youth's turbulence and the promise of the future. She fashioned the roots of resiliency and confidence in herself in the furnace of misfortune, her soul tempered by the light of truth and the flame of misunderstanding.

Elena set off on a voyage of self-discovery that day as her innocence clashed with the harsh realities of maturity, paving the way for knowledge and ignorance to yield to enlightenment. Through the trials of puberty, she discovered that although ignorance might plant the seeds of misinterpretation, knowledge, and comprehension can act as rays of light in the shadows, illuminating her way with bravery and resoluteness. Elena's perspective on the world also changed as a result of discovering the truth about sex and delivery; her knowledge grew beyond the boundaries of childhood innocence to encompass the complexity of maturity and the secrets of life itself.

The tragic incident shook Elena to her core. She felt a flood of grief rush over her as Miguel broke the news to her one fine day. How could Elena's own school have such cruelty on its premises? The town was left in a state of shock and dismay following the boy's sudden death. His parents departed to deal with the unimaginable loss of their only child and their seemingly unbeatable sadness.

As more facts emerged, the actual tragedy of the boy's bullying became apparent. Elena was unable to imagine the depths of his loneliness and anguish as he endured unrelenting suffering in silence. It served as a sobering reminder of the silent battles many kids fight beneath stiff exteriors and closed doors.

People were incensed as word of this horrible tragedy spread like wildfire. How could a life so young be snatched away with such cruelty? The boy's parents were inconsolable; they found it hard to comprehend that their lone kid had left them. The youngster had been the victim of bullying for a considerable amount of time, it was discovered throughout the course of the inquiry into the event. He was a calm, reserved youngster who lived alone. He was frequently observed sitting by himself in the school cafeteria, having no acquaintances. However, he never voiced his complaints or discussed the bullying with anybody, not even his parents.

When the boy's classmates were questioned, they disclosed that the bullies had pushed him about, teased him, and called him derogatory things. They even forced him to complete their assignments and threatened to hurt him if he didn't. However, the boy's self-advocacy was what ultimately caused them to lose patience. He smacked two of the bullies who were bothering him because he had had enough. The bullies were enraged by this and wanted revenge.

Tension flared in the air as the boy stood defenceless on the school building's terrace, surrounded by the bullies' frightening presence. The environment became more tense as they expressed animosity with their words and body language. There was a sudden fight in the middle of the conflict, which created a wild uproar. Amidst the turmoil, a bully acted impulsively and made a mistake, pushing the youngster over the roof. When they realized the permanent nature of what they had done, a collective cry of anxiety reverberated through the entire space.

The bullies were apprehended by the police and accused of murder. However, the harm had already been done, a family was destroyed, and a young life had been lost. All that remained for the boy's parents were recollections of their cherished kid.

The incident emphasised the seriousness of bullying and its potential consequences. It also highlighted how many kids suffer in silence because they're too scared to speak up. The fact that the school administration did not intervene sooner to stop the bullies was also criticized. Everyone was awakened by the boy's death, and measures were implemented to stop bullying in schools. In his honour, his parents established a charity to raise awareness of bullying and its consequences. The youngster may be dead, but his legacy will endure and his passing won't have been in vain.

Elena was shocked to learn that the bullies had used physical force in addition to verbal harassment, leaving her totally shocked. It was unexplainable how their savagery resulted in the needless death of a young person. Elena saw the boy's sad destiny as a sobering reminder of the uncertainty of life and the value of standing up to injustice. It strengthened her resolve to advocate for others as well as herself and to speak up for people who don't feel like they have a voice when faced with hardship.

Elena took the lessons she had learnt from the boy's premature death from the previous school with her as she started a new chapter in a new school, supported by her father's steady guidance. His passing will always serve as a poignant reminder of the critical need for understanding, compassion, and unity in the face of hardship.

Chapter - 7
Embracing Womanhood

The beginning of Elena's journey into womanhood was marked by subtle breezes of change, which murmured around her when she turned eleven. Her first experience with the faintest trace of crimson discolouring her underwear was on a calm afternoon, just like any other. This odd stain caused her little heart to race with wonder and doubt.

Elena was in her bedroom refuge, struggling with a range of emotions and trying to make sense of what was happening to her. Her mind was racing with questions and concerns. The gentle stirrings of rising in her soul blended with a wave of uneasiness.

Elena found consolation in her mother Carla's soft hug, which was accompanied by shaking hands and a fluttering heart. Carla's loving presence provided understanding and comfort during this uncertain time. Carla patiently and gracefully helped her daughter understand the many nuances of femininity, including the menstrual mysteries, by providing comfort and consolation via her sweet words.

Elena felt a mixture of fear and wonder in her heart as Carla talked; every word was a revelation, every explanation a window into the divine cycles of life itself. Her mother's soft voice offered comfort as she listened carefully, her little mind taking in the knowledge of earlier generations.

Elena discovered that she had gained knowledge and insight that helped her navigate the unfamiliar seas of puberty in the days that followed. Her movements took on the cadence of a silent symphony, the ageless dance of creation and regeneration echoed by subtle harmonics.

However, in the middle of the rumblings of change, Elena was overcome with a barrage of feelings, including anxiety, uncertainty, and a deep sense of vulnerability. The start of her period was a physical reminder of her journey from childhood to adulthood, which was filled with both excitement and fear.

Tracing the changes in her body, Elena struggled with the weight of cultural standards and social expectations as she faced the intricacies of her own identity. In a society that frequently associated femininity with weakness, she looked within herself for perseverance, bravery in the face of misfortune, and strength in her own vulnerability.

Elena saw the holy beauty woven into the feminine experience through the lens of her first period, a tapestry of elegance, courage, and unyielding determination. Every drop of blood was a silent affirmation of a woman's innate worth and strength, and a monument to the toughness of the female gender.

During the quiet times of reflection, Elena experienced a wide range of contradictory feelings, including dread combined with amazement and doubt mixed with optimism. But in the middle of her own heart's turmoil, she found a deep feeling of acceptance—acceptance of her own body, her own value, and the many opportunities that awaited her.

Elena took the knowledge of previous generations with her as she set out on her voyage of self-discovery, serving as a lighthouse illuminating the way to womanhood. She found comfort, strength, and a feeling of community in the slow beat of her monthly cycle, which served as a constant reminder that her body was a temple of holy beauty and divine grace rather than a source of shame or disgrace.

Elena discovered during her first period that being a woman was a journey rather than a goal. This path involved self-discovery, empowerment, and endless possibilities. And with a spirit enlightened by the ageless knowledge of centuries past, a soul flaming with possibilities, and a heart packed with courage, she set off into the unknown.

There was a special relationship between two homes in the DeSanta family's large neighbourhood, in the middle of the daily grind. Whenever Sarah's mother was abroad, the DeSanta home provided comfort to her as the daughter of Elena's friend. Sarah and Elena had a strong bond that went beyond simple proximity, even though their ages were different. Sarah used to frequently find herself in Elena's room, laughing late into the night and exchanging secrets. Their bond grew within the DeSanta home, a reflection of the openness and love that characterized their familial relationship.

Sarah was alone in her room one morning. Sarah sighed contentedly as she lay in bed, still reeling from the pleasure she'd had earlier in the day. Knowing that she had made a great start to her day, she couldn't help but smile.

But she found enjoyment in more than just the physical release. Giving herself pleasure gave her a feeling of empowerment and control. Sarah felt comfort in being able to openly explore her wants without criticism in a world where women were frequently chastised for their sexuality.

Sarah had always been interested in her body and the emotions it might arouse since she was a child. She recalled when she was a little child, slinking into her parents' room to try on her mother's silk nightgowns and seeing herself as an adult who understood the mysteries of pleasure. As she grew older, she was eager to discover the possibilities her body held. She opened her eyes slowly, sensing the warmth of the sun's rays on her skin through the drapes. But even with the soft warmth, she was unable to get rid of the restlessness that had been growing all morning. She could feel the yearning pulsing through her body and knew there was only one way to sate it.

She took a deep breath and reached down to the smooth fabric of her trousers, trailing her fingertips beneath the waistband. She started rubbing her clitoris in slow, gentle circles with a delicate, playful touch. She felt the first sparks of pleasure kindle within her and closed her eyes, letting out a faint groan.

Sarah's thoughts were racing, dreams and wants all focused on escape and pleasure. Her fingers kept exploring and tormenting her most private regions while she let her fantasies run wild. She shivered and moaned with pleasure as the plush material of her panties created an additional layer of sensation.

Sarah could feel the heat and wetness between her legs intensifying as she stroked and stimulated herself more. Her hips were grinding against her hand as her body reacted to her touch, yearning for more. Images of passion and ecstasy filled her mind, and she found herself indulging in them even further. Lost in the depths of pleasure, she pictured herself in a lover's arms. One possibility after another, each more tempting than the last, flashed across her head.

However, she was pushed to the brink by her own actions. She felt waves of ecstasy go through her body as her fingers danced over her clitoris. She was chasing the ultimate release, her motions more intense, her breaths more strained. Sarah eventually achieved her climax with one last, powerful rub. She trembled and gasped as a wave of pleasure swept over her. She lay there, glowing in the afterglow, and felt utterly content, even though her body was still trembling.

Sarah was on a steady downhill from her high, and all she could do was stare down at her hand in wonder. Even though she had always understood the power of self-love, she was constantly in awe of how amazing it might be.

Sarah got herself up and went back to bed, feeling pleased and at ease. She was aware that treating herself to a small act of self-love was the best way to begin the day. She couldn't wait to repeat the entire experience as she closed her eyes while still blushing and panting.

Sarah revealed what she had done to Elena that day. Elena, on the other hand, expressed her extreme displeasure at hearing Sarah's confession. Due to the gravity of Sarah's acts, Elena was unable to communicate with her friend because of an impenetrable barrier that seemed to exist between them. The emptiness where communication had previously flourished for a week served as a monument to Elena's sentiments. Because she was too young to comprehend, Sarah was left to consider the repercussions of her actions while the chasm between them, caused by her actions, hung heavy in the air and put a shadow over their bond. After just a week, Elena resumed normal interactions with Sarah, indicating a swift resolution to the discomfort she had initially felt.

Chapter - 8
Departing Echoes

The fabric of Elena's family became entwined with strands of both hope and doubt as time continued its unrelenting progression. Elena, now thirteen years old and in full bloom, was poised to enter adolescence, her heart burning with the prospect of fresh starts and uncharted journeys.

Her brother Diego, six years old, was a ray of sunshine, his laughter resonating through their house as he ventured into the world of schooling. He became taller, wiser, and more intrigued about the world outside their modest home with every day that went by.

The unwavering cornerstone of their family, Sofia, had set out on a path of her own that would take her past the gates of academics and into the wide realm of the working world. Equipped with fortitude and tenacity, she had surmounted the challenges of tertiary education, emerging victorious as a recently certified software engineer in the vibrant metropolis of Cape Town.

A tribute to the unwavering passion that flowed through their blood, Miguel, the patriarch of their family's tapestry, gleamed with pride as he saw his eldest daughter climb the edge of achievement. He opened their house to celebrate Sofia's successes, inviting friends and family to share in the happiness of her success, all with a heart full of appreciation.

However, despite the joyous celebrations, there was a faint hint of a shift in the air, which put doubt on the warmth of their family relationships. They had no idea that Sofia was hiding secrets of her own, goals and ambitions that drew her away from home and towards far-off places.

Sofia considered the route ahead of her in the deep recesses of her heart; it was a path full of possibilities but also a path full of uncertainty. She had a growing sense of unease about her family and a growing need for the freedom to explore and find herself as each day went by.

Sofia disappeared into the peaceful seclusion of her room as the sounds of laughing faded into the night, her mind drifting among the stars outside the windowpane. Feeling the weight of expectation pressing down on her, she made the decision to take control of her own fate and set off for the far-off land of liberty and self-government.

Thus, Elena's family found themselves at a turning point in history, their destiny entwined but on the edge of diverging, as the evening's flames faded and the stars silently kept watch overhead. With their spirits full of hope for tomorrow, their hearts unified in the face of uncertainty, they found comfort in the love links that held them together throughout the soft embrace of the night.

Sofia was the epitome of perseverance and hard work in the silent corners of their shared house, far from the last remnants of festivities and companionship. Her path, characterized by many giving ups and unshakable determination, had carried her to the highest level of achievement. But as time went on, her love for her family grew dimmer and dimmer, overtaken by the draw of far-off places and unexplored possibilities. Sofia struggled with the bittersweet reality that the journey to self-discovery frequently required farewells and fresh starts in the maze of her heart. So she set her sights on the unknown, her love for her family overshadowed by the limitless possibilities that awaited her outside of her home, a heavy heart in tow, and a soul longing for the freedom of the open road.

Sofia secretly wanted to extend her wings and take off for the far-off horizons of opportunity, but she kept this desire to herself in the tranquil recesses of their family paradise. She started a covert voyage, unaware of her family, driven by ambition's whispers and the hope of a better future.

Weeks passed and Sofia was still working nonstop, her days taken up by the never-ending quest for perfection. Her family had no idea that she was studying for an exam that would open doors to an infinite world where goals were called from a distance and ambitions danced on the edge of realization.

Sofia took on the enormous task head-on with unshakable determination, her spirit unfazed by the difficulties that lay ahead. She accomplished a remarkable feat of lightning-fast intelligence by passing the exam with an unwavering dedication that shone through any doubts.

The good news of Sofia's victory reverberated through their house, a glimmer of optimism among the jumble of their daily existence. But even as the family basked in the glory of Elena's achievement, the darkness remained deep within Elena.

Because of Sofia's rise to the highest level of achievement, Elena was left adrift in an ocean of doubt, and her sister's departure served as a sobering reminder of time's fleeting nature and change's inevitable course. Their relationship, which had previously been unshakeable, was now straining under the weight of secrets and silent grief.

The sisters' hearts were hurting from the weight of being apart and the anguish of things left unsaid when the discovery came to light, creating a rift between them. Elena battled the turbulent waves of emotion that threatened to overwhelm her fragile spirit because she was too young to understand the complexity of life's fabric.

The party that followed was a symphony of opposing feelings, an explosion of happiness and grief mixed together in the furnace of Sofia's leaving. Elena waited outside the celebration, silently crying and carrying a sad heart full of unspoken desire, as her family celebrated her newfound achievement. Elena desired to speak openly with her sister Sofia, but she couldn't.

When Elena was alone with her thoughts, she pondered the fleeting nature of human connection and the fragility of familial bonds. Through the prism of Sofia's departure, she discovered valuable lessons about the resilience of the human spirit and the art of letting go.

With the sounds of their departure echoing through their house, Elena found herself on the verge of a fresh start, her heart a kaleidoscope of mixed feelings, tinged with the sadness of saying goodbye and tinged with optimism. She learned the transforming value of resiliency and the lasting strength of familial bonds under the shadow of Sofia's departure, which helped her firmly ground her spirit on the beaches of love and memory.

Elena took comfort in the notion that family ties transcend time and geography, creating a tapestry of love and resiliency that continues through the changing of the seasons and the sands of time, even when the path ahead may be full of uncertainty.

Elena also discovered, as Sofia's departure came to pass, that her sister had been chosen to work as a software engineer at Google in California, USA—a credit to her diligence and unrelenting perseverance. Elena's heart remained heavy from the separation, her love for her sister a mute echo in the hallways of their shared memories, while the family celebrated Sofia's victory.

With her heart a beacon of hope among the darkness of uncertainty, Elena set out on a voyage of self-discovery following Sofia's departure, driven by the unshakable love of her family and the hope of a new dawn ahead.

Chapter - 9

Shadows of Betrayal

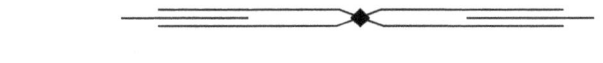

Elena's world, amid the maze-like hallways of her new school, was coloured with the hues of teenage dreams and blossoming love. She felt herself captivated by the mysterious appeal of youthful love, and her heart began to flutter gently, echoing the delicate dance of newly discovered feelings. However, a storm was building under the surface of her blossoming passion, threatening to tear apart the thin threads of her innocence.

Elena ventured to whisper the name of her beloved crush, Jake, a secret tucked away in the soft corners of her heart, to Chloe, her lone confidante. However, in the irrational world of adolescence, secrets were little more than murmurs conveyed by gossip that swept across their common haven like wildfire.

Unknowingly, Chloe's well-intentioned remarks set off a series of myths and accusations that brought Elena's personal emotions under intense public scrutiny. The news that spread about her love for Jake fueled the feelings of resentment and envy that simmered under the surface of their shared life.

Beneath the surface of dishonesty and fake friendliness, there was a sinister force lurking in the shadows amidst the pandemonium. Enraged and resentful, Ava used the chance to plant the seeds of dissension and wove a complex web of deceit and trickery to entangle Elena in its dark embrace.

Ava skilfully planned up a campaign of hate speech and slander, polluting the wellspring of friendship with her poisonous remarks. Casting Elena as the unintentional villain in her twisted story, she controlled the opinions of their peers like a puppet master tugging unseen strings. However, Ava's depravity had no boundaries since she went to the farthest lengths to spread hateful rumours about Elena, ruining her name with unfounded charges. Once a stronghold of knowledge and enlightenment, the school turned into a war zone of falsehoods and deceit, where reality was nothing more than a passing illusion.

Elena stood in the centre of the storm, her spirit tried by the furnace of hardship and her body beaten and wounded by the winds of treachery. Ava's falsehoods weighed heavily on her frail shoulders, obscuring her formerly hopeful disposition with uncertainty and hopelessness.

Elena found comfort in the arms of her family, whose steadfast love acted as a beacon of light in the darkest of nights, as the tendrils of sorrow tried to swallow her. Their words were a salve to her broken spirit, and their gentle care offered her safety from the storm. However, the betrayal left profound wounds that festered beneath the surface, destroying her confidence and hopelessness. There was no escape, not even in the classroom, where a teacher, blinded by prejudice and familial connections, unknowingly assisted Ava in her evil schemes.

Elena's once-bright eyes were darkened with terrible despair as the truth came to light, her confidence in justice crushed by the unforgiving hand of fate. The public's verdict on her innocence left her with scars that would forever tarnish her spirit, and injustice loomed big.

Elena was plagued by a number of health problems as the weight of betrayal weighed heavily on her frail heart. These ailments were a tangible manifestation of her anxiety and stress. Her days were ruined by crippling migraines that sapped her strength and energy, and her evenings were spent in bed, tormented by the ghost of hopelessness.

The storms of struggle had damaged but not shattered Elena's spirit as she battled uncertainty and sorrow in the quiet confines of the hospital room. However, in the middle of the gloom, a ray of hope briefly appeared, demonstrating the resiliency of the human spirit and the enduring force of love.

Elena thus came out of the crucible of adversity, her soul tempered by the flames of affliction and her determination fortified by the ties of friendship and family, while the echoes of treachery receded into the ether. Despite the potential for scars to persist, she came out stronger, her heart ablaze with hope for a new dawn.

Miguel, Elena's father, was a steadfast source of support and fortitude as she made her way through the perilous seas of teenage turbulence. After seeing his daughter's pain and suffering, Miguel decided to act independently and face the tempest that was raging within Elena's classroom.

Elena became entangled in a web of hopelessness and alone due to Ava's malicious spin on gossip and dishonesty. Elena's affection for Jake was accidentally revealed by Chloe, which Ava used as fuel for her evil plan and a weapon with callous disdain for the damage it caused.

Elena's world gradually collapsed around her as the burden of deceit and treachery pressed down on her frail soul. Her school's hallways, which had previously been a haven of knowledge and friendship, were now alive with rumours of disdain and mockery, each word a dagger pointed at her broken heart. Under the crushing weight of her suffering, Elena's health started to deteriorate as the rumours spread and doubts darkened her doorway. Her spirit, wounded but resilient in the face of misfortune, was a testament to the quiet wars fought within her soul, as evidenced by sleepless nights and pillows stained crimson from tears.

Miguel, her dependable guardian, came forward with unyielding resolve when she was at her lowest. Reaching out to the school with steely determination, he was a ray of reason in a world where turmoil threatened to swallow his daughter.

Miguel and Jake's father's encounter was characterized by a feeling of ease and relaxation, as well as an undercurrent of comfort and reassurance that eased any residual tensions or fears. It turned out that they were longtime friends. The unbreakable links of friendship between Miguel and Jake's father triumphed in the furnace of mutual concern for their kids, pushing aside the spectres of uncertainty and suspicion as their eternal companionship acted as a pillar of support among the chaos.

The veil of suspicion that hovered over Elena started to lift as the facts were exposed and the lies were refuted, exposing the innocence that was at the centre of her tortured heart. The harsh light of truth exposed Ava's duplicity, unravelling her web of lies and leaving behind nothing but the sour taste of regret. But in the middle of the uproar of disclosures and the subdued murmurs of forgiveness, Elena saw herself juggling a tempest of contradictory feelings. The teacher, who was formerly a pillar of strength and direction, said nothing in response to Ava's wrongdoings because of her partiality and familial ties.

Elena was faced with a dilemma after her father's intervention: she wanted to get past her small grudges that were threatening to break her soul, but she also wanted to forgive. Her heart was divided between wanting to lash out in rage.

Even yet, Elena took comfort in the unspoken link that had grown between her and Jake as the dust fell and the sounds of fighting vanished into the corners of her mind. They became friends through hardship, a ray of light in the gloom that lurked on the periphery of their world, brought together by the same hardships of their dads.

As they strolled hand in hand, their footsteps resonating down the shadowy hallways, Elena came to understand that even at the darkest moments, hope and restoration could still be found. Even while her wounds may be visible on the outside, they are a monument to the resilient spirit of a little child who refused to let life's hardships break her and act as a constant reminder of her inner strength.

Loneliness and hopelessness lurked in the tiny nooks of Elena's world, behind the surface of innocent childish play. She fought silent demons, struggling under the oppressive grip of worry and the weight of sadness, all while remaining unseen by those around her. Every morning was an uphill battle against the unrelenting flood of hopelessness, an alone voyage through her own mental maze.

Elena was alone and defenceless when she was bullied relentlessly, and the harsh words and deeds of her peers broke her fragile soul. Their disdain weighed heavy on her frail shoulders, leaving her adrift in a sea of loneliness and insecurity. Within the silent passageways of her heart, she harboured escape fantasies and brief glimpses of a world devoid of suffering.

But even in the shadows that threatened to engulf her, Elena did not waver in her quiet. She carried her responsibilities by herself, keeping her pain hidden from her family and friends' prying eyes. She hid her suffering deep inside, a quiet prisoner of her own hopelessness, out of fear of criticism and rejection.

Deep within Elena's thoughts lurked the spectre of suicide, a dark figure that seemed to be calling her to the edge. about her lowest points, she wondered about the appeal of forgetting, wishing she might be freed from the bonds of her pain. But even in the depths of her lowest point, she harboured a glimmer of optimism that served as a lighthouse in the middle of the approaching night.

Elena sought comfort in her family's loving embrace during her time alone; it served as a haven of warmth and compassion among the bitter cold of her hopelessness. Even though she never expressed how much suffering she was in, her parents' constant support was a quiet salve for her wounded spirit. Unspoken as it was, their affection around her was like a cocoon of protection, a haven from the internal tempest.

Elena gradually started to recover from the edge as the days grew into weeks and the weeks into months. She found little moments of calm and quiet in the soft rhythms of family life, a diversion from the never-ending chaos of her inner struggle. One small step at a time, she paved the way for recovery with the modest pleasures of silent moments of connection and laughter shared.

Miguel liked to remark, " Familia: donde la vida comienza y el amor nunca termina" for Elena. This meant family—the place where love never dies and life begins.

Elena took comfort in her father Miguel's love of vehicles amid the peace of their house. Miguel used to take Elena on long drives when she was feeling down. Elena used to adore lengthy rides. She would sit next to him and marvel as he worked beneath the hood, figuring out the workings of cogs and engines. Miguel's protective nature prevented her from driving even though she was itching to do so since it kept her safe from traffic hazards. However, despite her need, she took solace in their mutual passion, which served as a thread that united them in quiet understanding and woven throughout their connection.

Elena emerged from the depths of her sorrow as the shadows of despair faded, her soul tempered by the flames of hardship. Despite the wounds that continued to scar the terrain of her spirit, she greeted every day with a renewed sense of bravery and fortitude. She found the courage to face the obstacles ahead in the love of her family, knowing that she would never be completely alone on her path.

Chapter - 10
Unveiling Miguel's Secret Surfing

Elena, who usually uses her father Miguel's laptop for gaming, made a surprising discovery one day when perusing. She was intrigued by what she discovered and felt compelled to learn more. She was filled with both curiosity and unease as she made her way through the digital environment. She was unsure about whether to tell her father what she had discovered, and this gave an unexpected level of nuance to her usual laptop inquiry.

The graphic pictures on her father's laptop screen made Elena's heart accelerate. She had never before found a porn website, much less watched a film on it. But she couldn't take her eyes off of it because of something about how forbidden it all seemed. She selected a film that featured a guy and a lady in a poorly lit space. The man had a thick stubble on his chiselled jawline and was tall and powerful. In contrast, the woman had long blonde hair that fell down her back.

Elena observed the man drawing her closer to him and his lips meeting hers in a passionate kiss. Her heart raced because she could sense the burning desire and longing radiating from the screen. Squeezing her breasts and extending to her hips, the man's hands moved over the woman's entire body. With a sigh of ecstasy, the woman allowed the man's fingers to go down between her legs and tease her through her little knickers.

Elena noticed the woman's excitement increasing and her breathing getting more irregular, and her cheeks began to blush. When the man removed the woman's garment, lacy black bra and matching knickers were shown. Elena's admiration for the woman's flawless form was accompanied with a tinge of envy.

Now the man's hands were on her breasts, giving them a firm massage as he moved his lips down her chest and neck. Her breasts were free from his ravenous tongue as he undid her bra. Elena was in shock that she was witnessing this and that her body was reacting to what was happening in front of her.

The man's mouth slid lower, his tongue flicking over her stiffened nipples, as the woman's moans became louder. Elena couldn't help but feel a hint of envy mixed with excitement as she saw the woman's arousal gleaming on her knickers. The lady was a smooth, waxed mound that the man revealed as he pulled down her pants. Elena's eyes widened, seeing something she had never seen before—the woman's bareness. Without any delay, the man plunged in, his tongue caressing the woman's clit.

Elena watched the lady squirm and moan beneath the man's skilled touch, and her heart raced. She watched the woman's delight, feeling her own body heat up and her panties getting wet. The man then rose to his feet, his own desire showing through his trousers. Elena was astounded to see his large, thick member as he swiftly took off his clothing. She was curious and aroused at the same time because she had never witnessed a man's erection.

The woman gasped in ecstasy as the man moved to place himself between her legs and slowly penetrated her. Elena's body was reacting to what she was seeing, and she couldn't believe she was seeing this. She observed as the man pushed in and out of her while holding onto her hips with his hands.

The man picked up his speed, and the woman's cries became more intense. With each stroke, Elena could see the woman's body trembling with pleasure, and her own excitement increased. Although she couldn't believe she was genuinely attracted to this, she couldn't ignore the feelings pulsing through her body.

Then, as he entered her from behind, the man turned the woman over so that her chest was against the bed. Elena watched with wide eyes as the man's hand moved to her buttocks, his fingers playing with her hair. She was both, shocked and excited at the same time because she had never seen anything like this before.

The man's thrusts became fiercer and harder as he continued to touch the woman's back with his fingers. Elena saw the woman's groaning grow more fierce and powerful as her body sagged with pleasure. As the guy attained his climax, the lady experienced a strong orgasm that made her body quake. Elena heard the man pull out and unload himself on her back, his own cries of delight filling the room.

Elena sat there stunned, desire still pulsing through her body. Though she was shocked and intrigued by what she had just witnessed, she was unable to ignore it.

She closed the laptop and took a deep breath, trying to calm her racing heart. She knew she couldn't tell her father about what she saw, but she also knew that she would never be able to forget it. And as much as she tried to resist, she couldn't help but wonder what it would feel like to experience such passion and pleasure.

Chapter - 11
Blossoming Friendship

As the sun rose over the sleepy town, casting its golden rays upon the tranquil streets, Elena stepped out of her house, her backpack slung over her shoulder. Before she entered the busy hallways of her school, she believed it to be just another typical day.

One of her favourite voices shouted out to her above the normal commotion of laughter and chatting. Elena turned and noticed Jake smiling warmly, his eyes widening. Having greeted each other, she had no idea that they would soon be strolling side by side with harmonious footfall.

As the days stretched into weeks, Elena took comfort in her bond with Jake. They swapped tales, laughed together, and experienced the pure joy of friendship. Their relationship deepened with every second that went by, forming a web of mutual understanding and trust.

They took solace in one other's presence during lunch breaks, relishing the quiet moments of intimacy among the bustle of the school cafeteria. Their talks explored the depths of their common experiences and fantasies, veering between fact and fantasy.

Their bond became stronger outside of the classroom and beyond the walls of academia. Elena was greeted warmly as she entered Jake's realm, where she was surrounded by warmth and could hear laughing resonating through his house.

Together, they set out on adventures, discovering their town's secret treasures and journeying into unknown realms of joy and laughter. From expansive fields to vineyards, and horseback riding to leisurely walks, they delighted in the enchantment of recently formed friendships and the beauty of everyday life.

In the middle of the nuanced details of their developing connection, Elena will never forget this particular moment because it was so clear how much Jake understood and supported her. Before a sudden rush of agony hit Elena, it was just another day, but this one held a new challenge: Elena was about to experience her first menstrual day of the month. Jake was there for her through the ups and downs of puberty, a rock of support when she battled cramps and mood swings.

He dispelled the darkness of loneliness that threatened to consume her by providing a listening ear and a reassuring presence via silent empathy and gentle reassurance. Elena was so vulnerable that she sought comfort in the small act of being seen and understood, and the warmth of Jake's companionship helped to ease her concerns and uncertainties. And she realized that their relationship went beyond the parameters of typical friendship, rooted in the depths of shared experiences and steadfast support, as they sailed the uncharted seas of adolescence together.

Their family also woven themselves into the fabric of their friendship, laughing together and making memories that would last a lifetime. Elena discovered a sense of community among the jokes and friendship that she had never experienced before.

Elena and Jake stayed true to their friendship, its link strong enough to withstand the passing of time, when the seasons and winds carried whispers of change. When they had some alone time to ponder, Elena was struck by how beautiful their relationship was—a ray of hope among all the uncertainty in life.

Elena found the real meaning of friendship in the embrace of friendship—a symphony of cherished memories, unshakable support, and shared laughter. As they strolled hand in hand through the halls of teenage years, she was confident that their relationship would last, proving the strength of like souls finding comfort in one another's companionship.

Elena and Jake made a quiet pledge, their hearts intertwined in the soft beat of friendship—a link that would lead them through the challenges and victories that were ahead—as the sun sank on another day, throwing hues of gold and crimson across the horizon.

In the tender embrace of dawn's first light, a shadow fell upon Elena's family, casting them adrift in a sea of sorrow and despair. The resilient matriarch of their home, Tía Maria, carried the burden of her kids' dreams on her shoulders and used her heart as a stronghold to weather the storms of hardship. Her guiding lights on the darkest of nights were Isadora and Mateo, the very essence of her being.

However, fate unfurled its evil wings over their peaceful lives with no compassion, being cruel and unpredictable. The sound of tyres breaking apart and the icky crunch of metal hitting flesh broke the peace they had been living on a day much like any other. The void of senseless tragedy engulfed Isadora, tarnishing her purity with the heartless indifference of fate, her smile a beacon of hope, and her laughter a symphony of joy.

The details depicted a picture of hopelessness and sorrow, a tapestry of anguish engraved in the pages of sadness. Isadora, a young woman full of hopes and ambitions that had not come true, was lost in a reckless storm caused by the cowardice of an unidentified motorist. A tribute to the frailty of life's delicate dance, the streets, which had once been a playground of laughter and pleasure, were now filled with the silent echoes of pain and loss.

A fog of sadness covered them like a blanket as the news echoed through their house's hallways, constricting their breathing. Miguel was the one who had to deal the final blow, his voice quivering with anguish and his words a symphony of loss and shock. With her heart yearning for her daughter she could no longer embrace, Tía Maria's once-indomitable spirit was now broken by grief, and she sank beneath the weight of excruciating loss.

The shock of Isadora's death struck Elena more deeply than any weapon; the wound was infected with the poison of unmet goodbyes and unanswered inquiries. She struggled with the incomprehensible depths of loss in the quiet of her sadness, her tears a torrent of agony that threatened to drown her soul. The world, which had once been alive with hope for the future, was now enveloped in a cloud of melancholy that had dulled all of its colours.

The sorrow that weighed them down as they gathered to say goodbye to Isadora served as an anchor, binding them to the grim truth of death's harsh grasp. The funeral procession, a sombre march filled with tears and hushed prayers, served as a moving reminder of the transience of life's transient beauty and the value of each moment that passes.

Nevertheless, a light beacon glowed in the distance amidst the darkness, demonstrating the human spirit's tenacity in the face of overwhelming adversity. Even though Tía Maria was beaten, her faith remained firm despite all the hardships she faced. She found strength in the love that was all around her. She confronted the chasm with unwavering determination, her heart acting as a stronghold against the devastation of sorrow, with Mateo by her side.

Elena determined to honour Isadora's legacy, to treasure every moment as a priceless gift, and to never forget the incomparable brightness that she had given into their lives while her memory lingered like a ghost upon the wind. The everlasting ties of family provided her with comfort in the silent hallways of sadness, a lifeline in the face of the agony that threatened to swallow them all.

And Elena whispered a silent prayer for Isadora's restless spirit as the sun sank on another day, throwing dark shadows across their broken souls. Her voice was a symphony of grief and desire. The notion that love, unwavering and eternal, will lead them through the darkest of nights and serve as a beacon of hope among the approaching darkness gave her comfort in the twilight of despair.

As the echoes of tragedy reverberated through Elena's heart, she found herself ensnared in the suffocating grip of grief. She carried a heavy burden of grief from Isadora's passing, which left a shadowy trail in her dreams and thoughts. Her words were a fragile song that danced upon the winds of sadness, she found comfort in the tranquil shelter of Jake's presence.

Elena's voice trembled with the weight of untold sorrows as she spilt her agony to Jake, her face marred by tears and her heart burdened with grief. She talked of the broken world of Tía Maria, the premature hush of Isadora's laughter, and the yawning emptiness that accompanied them. And Jake wrapped his arms around her, providing a haven in the middle of the storm, even as the tears dropped like rain on the ground.

Elena could feel the steady cadence of Jake's heartbeat in the quiet of their mutual loss, a rhythm that kept her grounded. His touch, like a salve to her bruised heart, revealed a great deal about the unsaid love that united them. For a brief instant, in the middle of the tangled webs of grief and desire, Elena dared to believe that there may be a tiny bit of comfort in the middle of the chaos.

Time had tested their friendship, which had remained steadfast through it all and been a light in the darkest of nights. Both of their spirits had danced a delicate waltz of connection and trust, standing side by side in moments of both ecstasy and grief. However, there were hints of something more profound, something unsaid but very much there, beyond the surface of their platonic friendship.

Their family set out for the peak of the mountain one fatal day as the sun sank low in the horizon, turning the sky a fiery mix of gold and red. When Jake and Elena were lured to the edge of fate in the middle of the majestic beauty of nature's embrace, their hearts were exposed to the sky's watching eye.

Jake's voice broke through the silence in the silent seclusion of the mountain hug like a clarion cry, speaking words of unspoken passion. He knelt before Elena, his lips quivering and his heart exposed, his eyes burning with the fire of newly discovered resolution. And he said the words that would forever alter their lives at that timeless moment, amidst the soft rustle of the leaves and the whispering of the wind.

Elena's words lingered in the air like dewdrops sparkling in the early sun, her heart aflutter with a symphony of emotions as she stood frozen in time, the world around her slipping into darkness. She felt a spark light in her spirit at the suggestion, a confession of love forged in the furnace of shared moments and whispered hopes, pushing away the doubts and uncertainties.

Elena answered the question into the wind, her voice stifled by emotion and her hands shaking. Her words were a tribute to the unshakable trust that united them. And with the promise of tomorrow's dawn burning brightly in their hearts, Jake and Elena stood together in the glory of their newfound love as the sun sank below the horizon, throwing its last rays onto their intertwined figures.

In the words of Elena, "El amor no se mira, se siente"—that is, "Love is not seen, it is felt." This moving statement perfectly captures the notion that genuine love transcends outward looks and cursory judgments. It basically highlights the need for emotional understanding and connection in relationships and the fact that true love is derived from the heart and soul rather than just appearances.

Their souls permanently entwined in the tapestry of destiny's embrace, they set off on a voyage of love and adventure at that timeless moment, among the hushed whispers of the mountain air. And they realized, looking down at the enormous expanse of the globe below, that they could withstand any storm that dared to come their way as a team.

Elena and Jake crafted a tapestry of cherished memories and unsaid vows in the mosaic of their entwined lives, with each strand demonstrating the depth of their bond. With each day that went by, their relationship became stronger as they made their way through the maze of adolescence and persevered through the high school years.

In the crowded hallways of their school, rumours circulated behind them, highlighting their developing relationship. Ava was among those whose jealousy was simmering under an appearance of indifference, even though many others looked at them with admiration. Ava's heart ached from unfulfilled yearning as she looked at Jake with such penetrating eyes and gave subtle digs.

However, Elena and Jake persisted in the face of Ava's unspoken bitterness, their love a ray of hope among the darkness of uncertainty and envy. Elena awaited Jake's every move on the football pitch as he skillfully manoeuvred around the opposition, his teammates and Elena's loving eyes celebrating each of his goals.

Nights of shared closeness slid into evenings as they sought solace in the warmth of one another's embrace. Their laughing sounded like the melody in the darkness as they laughed themselves silly in the warm embrace of their shared space over movie marathons and late bites.

Elena and Jake ventured out from the well-known streets of their neighbourhood to explore the vivid Soweto tapestry and the busy metropolis of Johannesburg. Walking hand in hand, they enjoyed the diverse fusion of cultures as they strolled through busy marketplaces and quiet lanes.

Their relationship blossomed during the calm times of study sessions and test preparation, their thoughts fusing in a dance of mutual support and shared knowledge. Together, they overcame the difficult obstacles of academia, their resolve remaining strong in the face of difficulty.

And they stood as a single, cohesive force rather than as individuals when the results of their labour were eventually seen, their victory a monument to the strength of commitment and love. They knew that no matter what challenges awaited them, they would overcome them as a pair, hand in hand, their hearts entwined in a connection that cut over time and distance.

From the beginning of their adventure, Elena and Jake's love was more than just a passing feeling; it was a deep bond that held them together. In their views, love was an intangible sensation that was experienced via the heart; it was a guiding force that helped them navigate life's ups and downs, providing constant illumination along the way.

When Elena took time to think quietly, she frequently discovered that she was amazed by the strength of their relationship and felt appreciative of Jake's constant support and company. Because of their love, they were able to find courage and comfort in the middle of life's turbulent waves in a world full of uncertainty.

Elena and Jake realized as they stood on the edge of the future that their love would be their beacon of hope, holding them steady and graceful through all of life's curveballs. Armed with each other's strength and support, they bravely and resolutely approached the unknown, certain that they could overcome the difficulty that lay ahead.

With their hearts full of optimism and their spirits burning brightly from their love, they ventured off into the wide unknown together, hand in hand. They discovered a home and a place to withstand any adversity, becoming stronger and closer than before, in one another's arms.

Chapter - 12
Exploring California's Wonders

One bright morning, in the middle of their regular routine, Elena's father, Miguel, decided on the spur of the moment to take the whole family to California to visit their daughter, Sofia. This choice sent a shockwave through the family. Miguel inspired the group with a big smile and a glimmer of joy in his eyes. He made reservations for travel to the Golden State and excited everyone about what was ahead.

Elena sensed the thrill of adventure radiating from her family as they boarded the plane and felt a flutter of excitement developing within her breast. Her mother Carla was a rock and a source of strength for her father Miguel. Her maternal presence warmed and comforted their family's dynamic. Diego, her younger brother, was by her side; his contagious grin and inexhaustible energy brought a humorous spark to their trips.

They were excited to see Sofia again after she had travelled far to follow her ambitions, so they talked and had a great time on the journey to California. Heartswelling with anticipation for the memories they would make as a family, Elena dreamed of the adventures that awaited them in the country of sunshine and dreams.

Elena's family was excited and looking forward to what lay ahead as the jet dropped over the wide state of California. Her mother, Carla, was holding Elena's hand tightly and her eyes were beaming with delight while her father, Miguel, leaned forward in his seat and peered out the window with keen expectation. Younger brother Diego, full of restless energy and eager to explore their new surroundings, bounced in his seat.

Elena and her family felt as though they had entered a dream when they arrived in California. As they got off the plane, the warm embrace of the California sun engulfed them, making them feel amazement and warmth in their hearts. After being apart for seasons and miles, Sofia's warm grin welcomed them to the airport, and her delight mirrored theirs.

Their first destination was the vibrant metropolis of Los Angeles, a place full of opportunity and life. Elena felt her veins race with adrenaline as they got off the plane and onto the tarmac. Her father, who was usually the one to plan things out, had carefully planned their schedule so he could show his family all the attractions in the city. Every area of Los Angeles, from the famous palm-lined streets of Beverly Hills to the free-spirited atmosphere of Venice Beach, has something fresh to explore.

As they passed the dazzling lights of Hollywood, Elena's eyes became wide with amazement. The famous sites of the Walk of Fame and the Grauman's Chinese Theatre captured her attention. To preserve their memories of this amazing voyage, her mother avidly took pictures, documenting every moment. Diego asked his tour guide a lot of questions, his joy contagious and his eyes beaming with delight.

Elena was charmed by San Francisco's distinct charm and character as they travelled even farther north. As they entered the city, the Golden Gate Bridge's imposing silhouette welcomed them, its rust-coloured spans vanishing into the haze. As Elena strolled through Chinatown's narrow lanes, she was astounded by the vivid lantern displays and the enticing smells of dim sum that permeated the neighbourhood.

The magnificent national parks of California, with their towering redwoods reaching the sky and tumbling waterfalls into glistening pools below, were traversed by them throughout their voyage. Elena was filled with tremendous astonishment and wonder as she stood among Yosemite's old giants, their majestic presence overwhelming her. Her father led them on adventures into the pristine forest, his love of the natural world clear in every step. He had always been an outdoorsman.

Elena and her family enjoyed the relaxed environment and endless stretch of immaculate beaches along Southern California's sun-kissed coastline. Making sandcastles and splashing in the soft Pacific Ocean waves characterized their carefree afternoons. They spent their evenings together over beach bonfires, toasting marshmallows and chatting late into the night.

That was not the end of their experience. With its breathtaking cliffs and towering sequoias of Yosemite National Park, California enticed travellers with its natural treasures. Hiking down rough paths, they were treated to beautiful views that went on forever, as well as waterfalls that sprang out. They relished every second of the golden hour as they watched the sunset over the undulating hills of wine country and put their toes in the glistening waters of Lake Tahoe.

But even in the middle of the opulence of the metropolis and the magnificence of the natural world, Elena and her family were most affected by the little things in life. They picnicked beneath the towering redwoods, indulged in artisanal delicacies at the Ferry Building Marketplace, and had freshly caught seafood at Fisherman's Wharf. They also realized that their trip to California will always be a treasured memory as they watched the sun, set and paint the sky in pink and gold hues.

The diversity and splendour of California enthralled Elena and her family throughout their tour. Every minute was full of exploration and excitement, whether it was in the peaceful woods or the busy streets of the metropolis. Elena brought memories from their time spent in the Golden State with her, serving as a monument to the endless splendours of California.

The trip home from California was an emotional trek across the terrain of recollections, with every mile serving as a quiet conduit between the spheres of happiness and sadness that had characterized their stay in the Golden State. Elena's mind wandered back to the sun-kissed beaches and busy city streets that had provided the setting for their family's journey as the jet took off into the clear blue sky. However, beyond the surface of exhilaration that had preceded their trip to California, there was a deep sense of loss - an observable absence that mirrored the space created by Sofia's departure.

Hour by hour, the reality of their return voyage sank in, lowering their once-bright spirits to a sombre tint. Elena found it difficult to accept the idea of leaving behind the golden beaches and majestic redwoods of California; it served as a sad reminder of how fleeting their time together as a family was. Her heart hurt for the moments of connection that had kept them together despite the expansiveness of the Golden State, for the laughter and companionship they had shared.

Elena was surrounded by a sea of faces as they exited the aircraft and moved through the busy airport terminals, each one serving as a quiet reminder of how fleeting their trip was. She was heartbroken by Sofia's absence, which threw a pall over their return to reality as they made their way through the hordes of exhausted and sorrowful travellers.

Back home, the memories of their time spent as a family filled each room, and the echoes of their California journey echoed through the corridors of their home. Still, there was a hint of nostalgia in the comfortable settings, a yearning for the warmth of Sofia's soft presence and the laughter that their house had once been filled with.

With the gloom in the air, Elena's mind went to Jake, her reliable partner and confidante. She wanted nothing more than to tell him her stories of adventure and to relive their time together in the country of dreams and sunlight. Elena headed for Jake's house with a mixed feeling of regret and excitement, wanting to see her friend again and bring the warmth of their relationship to fill the hole left by Sofia's departure.

However, Elena was taken aback when she entered Jake's well-known surroundings. Instead of his normally upbeat attitude, Jake's eyes were filled with melancholy. Elena stepped closer to him warily, feeling that something was off. She was confused by his abrupt shift in attitude.

Jake, who was filled with sadness, said that his melancholy was due to his approaching departure for the UK, where his uncle lived, to complete his 11th and 12th grades. Elena's aspirations of keeping their relationship the way it had always been destroyed by the news, which struck like an infinite number of bricks. Elena was left reeling from a deep feeling of loss as the possibility of Jake being away from her for the next two years clouded their once bright future together.

As the day of Jake's departure approached, Elena struggled with a range of feelings, including grief, anxiety, and a deep-seated need for his consolation. Even yet, there was a calm resolution to treasure the times they had together and look forward to the day they would be together again, even in the middle of the chaos. Elena held onto the hope that their relationship would remain despite the distance separating them as she navigated the bittersweet currents of parting for the time being.

Chapter - 13
Jake's Departure: A Bittersweet Adieu

Elena's thoughts were racing with opposing feelings as she struggled with Jake's imminent departure and the unpredictability of their relationship's future. She felt as though she was adrift in a sea of uncertainty, her worry growing with every passing instant. She had a sad heart because she realized she had to face the urgent necessity to close the growing gap between them.

Gathering her bravery, Elena decided to address the problem directly. Step by step, her heart pounded as she made her way to Jake's residence. A surge of anxiety swept over her as she got closer to his front door, threatening to engulf her resolve. But she persisted, understanding that she had to stop letting fear control her.

Inside, Jake's possessions were scattered carelessly over the room, surrounded by the remains of his life. His eyes flickered with a mixture of surprise and confusion as Elena arrived, and he looked up. She could feel their unsaid thoughts hanging there, weighing them down, entwining them in a web of mutual anxiety.

They both struggled with the weight of the things they chose not to say as they fell into an uncomfortable quiet. Elena was aware that they couldn't avoid the problem indefinitely, though. She forced herself to speak, voicing the anxieties that had been eating away at her heart.

Elena said, her voice quivering a little from emotion, "I don't know how we're going to make this work, Jake. The thought of being apart from you for so long...it's tearing me apart."

As he extended his hand to take hers, Jake's demeanour softened and his eyes became sympathetic. With remorse in his voice, he said, "I know, Elena. I've also been giving it some thought. There is no question that it will be difficult."

They sat silently together for what seemed like an eternity, debating the gravity of their mutual problem. But in the middle of the confusion, some clarity started to show. Encouraged by a common resolve, they started to discuss the notion of temporarily ending their partnership and allowing each other to follow their own courses free from expectations.

They discussed for a long time before coming to a resolution. They decided to pause their love affair and turn it into a friendship with sorrowful hearts. Even though it was a challenging decision, they felt it was the right one under the current situation. Making the choice was tough since it was tinged with loss-related anxiety and uncertainty. Nevertheless, they both felt in their hearts that, in the circumstances, it was the correct decision. Elena shook her head in agreement, her eyes full of unshed tears despite her sad heart.

Elena felt a wave of resignation pass over her as they shared a final, heartbreaking embrace. She was aware that the moment they parted, a new chapter full of difficulties and unknowns had begun in their lives. However, she also understood that regardless of how far away they were, their relationship would endure the test of time.

Elena made the decision to immerse herself in an unfamiliar hobby as a means of trying to block out the agony of their separation. In the same vein as her brother Diego, she enrolled in a lawn tennis teaching program. She was able to redirect her emotions into something constructive because of the enjoyable diversion that the exercise offered.

The following day, both families gathered at the airport to say goodbye to Jake. Knowing that this farewell was the start of a new chapter in their life, Elena tried not to cry as she gave him a strong hug. They promised to stay friends and stay in touch despite the grief of their separation, hoping that their paths might cross again in the future. They were embarking on different routes for the time being, but she was confident that their love would persevere and serve as a lighthouse to get them through the darkest of nights.

As the days turned into weeks, and weeks into months, Elena was left struggling to deal with Jake's departure from her life. They'd promised to be friends, but as their hectic schedules drew them to opposite places, their chats got fewer and further between. His departure had created a vacuum that felt difficult to fill.

Elena's world appeared to get smaller every day as the weight of loneliness and desire cast a shadow over her once-vibrant existence. But in the middle of all, she felt a glimmer of strength that propelled her forward and inspired her to construct a new route for herself.

Her father Miguel would frequently take her on spontaneous rides in the evenings, the vast expanse of open road before them like a blank canvas ready to be filled with their memories together. Elena was engulfed in a sense of serenity as he carefully led her through the nuances of driving, the constant hum of the engine soothing her anxieties into submission.

But Elena soon discovered that becoming a proficient driver wasn't a simple task and that there were many obstacles in her way. Every session presented a fresh set of challenges to conquer, from learning the careful balancing act between clutch and accelerator to negotiating the chaotic labyrinth of city streets. Elena still met each obstacle head-on and did it with elegance and drive thanks to Miguel's tenacious coaching and unfailing support.

But even though she made every attempt to keep herself occupied, Jake's ghost continued to haunt her, serving as a continual reminder of their former friendship. There were brief moments of connection between them during their infrequent chats, but time appeared to be separating them more and more.

The sound of tennis balls hitting the court dominated her evenings, and the repeated motion of her racket served as a pleasant diversion from the upheaval in her emotions. She took up the sport alongside her brother Diego, intending to become an expert player and find comfort in the comforting rhythms of the game. She discovered that she was forming unanticipated relationships with her fellow tennis lovers. Elena found a sense of friendship and belonging that she hadn't realized she was lacking because of their mutual love of the sport, which served as a foundation for friendships.

In an attempt to restore her feeling of normalcy, Elena immersed herself in her academic endeavours and extracurricular activities, finding solace in the companionship of new acquaintances and the comforts of ritual. They were a pleasant diversion from the pain of loneliness that was about to overwhelm her, and she took comfort in their laughing and company.

Elena sensed her strength and resilience increasing daily in the face of hardship. Accepting that these changes were an essential component of her path to self-awareness and development, she started to welcome the changes that were taking place inside of her. Despite the unknown, she confronted the path ahead with renewed resolve, confident in her ability to overcome whatever obstacles that lay ahead.

So Elena continued to follow the curves of her life's ever-changing course, her heart full of optimism for the future and the prospect of fresh starts on the horizon, as the days grew into weeks and the weeks into months. There were plenty of challenges and unknowns in store for her on the road ahead, as she could see as she glanced towards the horizon. Yet she also understood this, equipped with the knowledge and connections she had made along the road, she was prepared to take them on head-on.

The core of Elena's development and evolution throughout time is captured in this chapter, which represents her path of self-discovery and determination in the face of hardship.

Elena's life was beginning to resemble a typical one. Her studies were going well, she had made new friends, and as she got more engrossed in her daily routine, her thoughts of Jake started to wane. But underneath the apparent peace of her life, a storm was building that might potentially upend the delicate harmony she had spent so much time nurturing.

Elena was faced with a reality she could never have anticipated on what appeared to be an average day. She was completely shocked to discover a web of lies when she asked to borrow her father Miguel's phone so she could send a message to her mother Carla. Her heart fell as she read through his texts and saw that Miguel was having private chats with another lady, exchanges that seemed to hint at an undercover affair.

Elena was overcome with shock as she processed the magnitude of what she had found. A million questions rushed through her head, each one more disturbing than the previous. How could their father, the head of the household, so blatantly betray their mother? And what did this realization signify for the future of their family?

Amidst her chaos, Elena had to make a challenging decision. Should she approach her father and run the danger of causing the fragile family unit to come apart? Should she remain silent and bury the truth deep in her heart in order to hold onto the false sense of bliss that her father's lies had destroyed?

Her decision weighed heavily on her and threatened to suffocate her due to its enormity. She knew that revealing her father's affair would permanently change their family's dynamic, so on the one hand, she was afraid of the consequences. However, the idea of her mother being ignorant and her trust being betrayed by the one person she had supposed to be steadfastly faithful to was too much for her to handle.

Elena ultimately had to make a decision, and it was motivated by her wish to save her family more suffering. She made the decision to hide Miguel's betrayal from the world, burying the truth deep in her heart to save her mother from the destruction that would undoubtedly result if it were revealed.

However, uncertainty began to chew at the edges of her determination even as she made her choice. Had she been wise to hold onto Miguel's secret? Or had she allowed the affair to go unchecked, subjecting her family to a lifetime of lies and mistrust?

Elena struggled to get over the notion that she had joined her father in his treachery and had become a silent collaborator to his lie as she struggled with shame and doubt. However, she secretly harboured the thought that maybe certain secrets were better left unseen because their realities were too painful to face.

Therefore, bearing the burden of her father's secret, Elena set off on a self-exploration trip in which she wrestled with the intricacies of love, loyalty, and the links that bound their family together. With hopelessness, she looked for the light to help her navigate the darkness cast by her father's deception, believing that eventually, they would return to the truth.

This chapter examines the dilemma of morality that Elena encounters after learning of her father's cheating as well as the fallout from her choice to keep him a secret. Highlighting the significant influence that secrets may have on the links that bind us together, it explores themes of loyalty, lying, and the complicated nature of family relationships.

Chapter - 14
A New Rival, A New Friend

A year had passed since Jake's departure, and Elena had become comfortable in her routine. She would spend her mornings studying, and her nights on the tennis court, where she would hone her talents and enjoy the challenge of competition. She could immerse herself in the beat of the match and the companionship of her fellow players on the tennis court, which had become her haven. She saw that as the weeks went by, she was becoming better and better every practice session because of her commitment and enthusiasm.

As the sun sank low in the sky one fateful day, Elena was put up against Paxton, an unfamiliar opponent. She could tell he was confident from the time he went onto the court because of his smooth and controlled warm-up motions before the match. Elena was intrigued by his air of cool determination, and she couldn't help but get a little excited yet terrified about the possibility of taking on someone as strong as him.

Elena saw early on in the encounter that Paxton was not to be taken lightly. He easily outmanoeuvred her across the court with his strong and accurate strokes, each landing with perfect accuracy. Elena tried her hardest to stay up, but she was unable to, and her irritation increased with every point she dropped. Even yet, she couldn't help but be in awe of Paxton's dexterity and talent during the intense game, as his grasp of the game was apparent in every move.

Paxton won, and it was a well-deserved triumph as the bout came to an end. Elena was unhappy about losing, but she also had a lot of respect for her opponent. She was captivated by his calm confidence and steady focus because of his humility in winning and his generosity towards her. His actions said volumes about his character.

Following the game, Paxton walked over to Elena and offered her a kind smile and a sportsmanlike handshake. He remarked, "Well played," in a straightforward but sincere tone, praising her efforts on the court.

Grateful for his words of kindness, Elena smiled back at him, still struggling to gather her breath after the intensity of the battle. She knew she had learned a lot from the confrontation, even if she had lost, and she was proud to have taken on such a strong opponent.

Over the next several days, the mutual passion they had for the game brought Elena and Paxton closer together. After the practice, they started to hang out more, talking tactics and skills well into the night. Although they were fierce rivals when playing, their love of tennis helped them to become close friends off the field.

Elena saw that she was becoming more and more close to Paxton every day, and their friendship was expanding in ways she had not anticipated. She was moved by his quiet strength and resolve, and she respected his devotion to the game and his persistent pursuit of perfection.

Elena couldn't help but be excited for the voyage that awaited them as they started this new chapter of their life together. She was excited about the experiences they would have both on and off the tennis court because she felt that everything was possible when Paxton was at her side.

So, as another day came to an end, Elena was overcome with thankfulness for the unanticipated bond that had developed between her and Paxton. She was certain that her bond with him would only get stronger over time since she had discovered in him not only a worthy rival but also a faithful friend and companion.

With the events of this phase, Elena and Paxton will form a new bond that will influence their lives in ways they never would have predicted.

As the days turned into weeks, Elena had to walk a tightrope between her friendship with Paxton and something more. He was a source of buoyancy in every contact, but underneath the surface of their developing relationship, there was a lurking doubt. She was starting to sense a connection with Paxton, but she couldn't get rid of the persistent fear that his goals might not be the same as hers.

One very calm evening at the tennis court, Elena waited anxiously while Paxton warmed up for his last match of the day. She had been used to their post-practice chats and was looking forward to getting out of the court and spending time with him. But when Paxton stepped closer to her, his serious gaze fell on her as he broke the news.

"I've decided to sign up for some graphic design classes," he said, reconsidering his choice. "I'll be leaving early from now on."

The news gave Elena a twinge of regret, as the idea of their time together coming to an end crushed her aspirations for their developing bond. She was aware of how important Paxton's studies were, yet she still felt sad about the passing of their regular conversations. She had become used to their exchanges, finding comfort in his words and consolation in his company.

In the days that followed, Elena struggled to accept the possibility that Paxton might not feel the same way about her. She yearned for their relationship to become stronger, but she couldn't get rid of the impression that Paxton was more interested in other things. He was devoted to his work; he gave his studies and his game his whole attention, making little space for other interests.

Elena felt lost in an ocean of doubt as their communications got more and more irregular due to Paxton's rigorous schedule. Social media allowed them to stay in touch, but Paxton's absence on the tennis court created an emptiness that was hard to replace. She missed their shared easy companionship, simple chats, and easy laughs.

Elena couldn't help but wonder whether she had misinterpreted the clues and that her feelings for Paxton were just idle thoughts as she thought back on their time together. She had a slight sense of shame due to her openness, her emotions exposed to someone who might not have returned her feelings.

Her heart ached with a sense of loss when she found that Paxton had completely dropped out of the coaching session. She was saddened by the breakup of their friendship even though she understood his reasons for going. Realizing that not all relationships were destined to last was a painful realization.

However, Elena saw a ray of optimism within the sorrow of their parting. Her knowledge of the nature of connection and the significance of knowing one another had grown significantly. Even with the wounds to her heart, she was still willing to consider making new acquaintances and starting over. It was a monument to the fragility and beauty of human connection that she knew she would always have the memories of her time with Paxton with her as she looked to the future.

Elena's emotional journey is explored in depth in this chapter as she struggles with unfulfilled sentiments and the painful realisation that not all relationships are intended to stay. It acts as a moving reminder of the difficulties in forming meaningful relationships with others and the resiliency of the human spirit in the face of loss and despair.

With just the soft murmurs of the night to accompany her, Elena was left floating in a sea of uncertainty and hopelessness in her lonely chamber. With each wave smashing relentlessly against the borders of her consciousness, her thoughts raced through her head like a whirlwind. She wondered why life seemed to be so cruel and why the world had chosen her to suffer as she struggled with the weight of her emotions.

"Why is it always me?" she said, her voice almost audible above a whisper. "Why do people walk away carelessly and without expressing anything? What have I done to merit this never-ending circle of suffering and grief?"

She thought about how her extended family was broken apart and how she had felt alone and alone because of the conflicts inside her own family. Her relatives were broken beyond repair, and even though she yearned for the comfort of family, she discovered herself cut off from them. She loved her cousin Isadora, who was taken from her way too soon, but she had never really bonded with any of her cousins before.

She said, her voice shaking with passion, "I miss you, Isadora," into the darkness. I miss our private whispering under the stars and our shared laughing. How come you have to part from me here on Earth alone?"

Then her mind went to Sofia, her beloved sister who seemed to be getting more and farther away from her every day. Though Sofia yearned for a relationship, she stayed aloof, prioritizing her own life above their familial relationship. Although Elena was desperate to connect with her and close the distance between them, she couldn't bear to think of bothering her sister with her suffering.

"I love you, Sofia," she said, her words a subtle request for comprehension. "I wish you were here to envelop me in your arms and drive away the darkness that haunts my dreams. Why did you decide to put your goals ahead of your sister?"

Elena felt the old feeling of loneliness nibbling at her heart as she lay in the darkness, the weight of her loneliness crushing down upon her. She didn't have many pals with whom to confide or with whom to discuss her troubles. She really wanted to tell her parents everything, but she couldn't face the idea of putting them through her suffering since their love for her was too valuable to endanger.

Her thoughts drifted to the ghosts of her past, frightening reminders of the heartbreaks she had experienced, as she sat in the solitude of the night. Jake's leaving hung huge in her mind, an open wound that would not go away even after all this time. She felt a hollow aching that reverberated deep inside her as a result of his absence.

"Why did you leave, Jake?" Her voice tinted with regret, she spoke into the darkness. "Did I fall short?"

The anguish of his absence was a continuous companion in her day-to-day existence, as her heart grieved at the thought of their parting. Even though they had agreed to stay friends, they didn't talk much as the days went into weeks and the weeks into months. The relationship they had previously had appeared to be disintegrating at the margins, its delicate threads coming apart every day.

In the midst of her loneliness, Paxton appeared like a glimmer in the darkness. Though short in duration, his influence on her life was profound, serving as an important example of how brittle human relationships can be. Because of his insightful character and calm manner, she had been pulled to him. During her lonely moments, their talks had provided her with a temporary break from the internal conflicts.

However, Paxton had escaped her grasp, and his exit left her feeling more isolated than before. It had come as a shock when he decided to quit instructing tennis in favour of taking graphic design classes, a clear reminder of how fleeting their relationship was. She knew how important his studies were, but she couldn't help but become a little upset when she thought about him being gone.

Thus, her heart was burdened by the weight of her feelings as she found herself adrift in a sea of grief. Her despair became more and more evident with every instant that went by, its gloomy melodies resonating throughout the depths of her being. But in the middle of the shadows, a glimmer of insight lighted her way—a subtle but profound truth that spoke to her soul.

Elena's voice resounded quietly in her room as the sorrowful song slowly influenced the air, her voice scarcely more than a whisper in the silence of the night. "Cuando eres feliz, disfrutas la música. Pero, cuando estás triste, entiendes la letra," she murmured, her words carrying the weight of her emotions. Translated, they meant: "When you are happy, you enjoy the music. But, when you're sad, you understand the lyrics." With each syllable, she found herself drawn deeper into the poignant truth of those words, a bittersweet reminder of the profound connection between music and emotion.

Elena had a moment of illumination when she understood that her suffering was a gift rather than a punishment. She developed a stronger empathy for the human experience as a result of her pain, which was brought about by her personal struggles. And even though the path ahead would be difficult, she was confident that she would overcome them with bravery and resiliency, her heart strengthened by the awareness that she was never really alone, even at her lowest points.

This chapter explores the depths of Elena's sadness as she struggles with the weight of her emotions, diving into her intense sense of loneliness and isolation. It is a moving reminder of the pain that all people feel on a regular basis and the transformational potential of empathy and understanding.

In the hush of the night, Elena felt overwhelmed by her sorrows and longed for a break from the darkness that surrounded her. She decided to go on a midnight expedition, a lone voyage into the uncharted depths of the night, in an attempt to improve her mood.

Elena walked carefully down the quiet hallways of her house, mindful not to wake the sleeping residents, a sense of purpose propelling her onward. As she moved towards the corridor where the keys to her escape lay, the soothing brightness of the moon created ethereal shadows that guided her movements.

Elena reached for the keys, pulse-pounding, but her fingers remained firm and the cool metal felt comforting in her grasp. Slipping through the door silently, she stepped out into the cool embrace of night, the darkness surrounding her like a comfortable cloak. Except for the wind's soft whispering through the trees, everything outdoors was enveloped in an unsettling silence. Elena saw that the anxiety she had been carrying was starting to fade with each step and was replaced with excitement for the adventure ahead.

Elena stopped for a time as she got closer to the car that was parked in the driveway because she was full of uncertainties and anxieties. She had never driven by herself before with nobody on the seat beside, and certainly not at night, when the stars were her sole source of guidance. However, the allure of the wide road drew her in, imploring her to let go of her worries and seize the independence that lay ahead.

Elena took a deep breath and got behind the wheel, her fingers shaking a little as she turned on the engine. She prayed softly as she turned the key, and the engine purred comfortingly to life. She held her breath for a brief while, worried that the noise might startle her parents out of their sleep, but the night went on without incident, her covert mission hidden in the shadows. A feeling of excitement filled her as she carefully steered the car onto the empty streets, the excitement of being on the open road pulsing through her body. She followed her instincts and wound her way through the little streets, feeling free for the first time.

Elena lost herself in the beat of the road as soothing music played in the background, the car's subtle swing lulling her into a delightful state of peace. There was just the pure joy of spending time by herself thinking as the night's reassuring embrace around her. There were no expectations or judgements. With the thrill of the night heightening her senses, Elena felt fully alive for the first time in what seemed like an eternity. As she pushed the car to its limits and floated along abandoned back roads and vacant highways, the wind whipped across her hair.

Elena became engrossed in the cadence of the journey, her anxieties about the outside world dissipating with every mile that went by. She felt as though she were flying on the wings of her newfound liberation, temporarily released from the weights that had been weighing her down. She spent hours driving with no direction or destination in mind, letting the meandering roadways lead her on a voyage of self-realization and relaxation. Elena experienced a calmness that swept over her as the first rays of early morning appeared over the horizon, her heart feeling lighter than it had been for some weeks.

Elena unwillingly drove the car back towards her house as the first rays of natural light began to show up on the horizon, her heart heaving at the thought that her night-time adventure was coming to an end. After parking the car in the driveway, she cautiously made her way back into the home, keeping her covert adventure a secret from everyone but the stars overhead.

Elena sighed contentedly as she fell asleep, her concerns lightened by the recollection of her nocturnal escape. She drifted off into visions that promised fresh starts and many opportunities as sleep took her.

The nighttime expedition that Elena embarks on to find peace in the freedom of the open road is captured in this chapter, which also highlights her journey of self-discovery and release. It represents her need for escape and her search for inner serenity in the middle of her emotional storm.

Chapter - 15
A New Path Begins

In the midst of the chaos of her final year of high school, her 12th-grade. Elena was struggling to deal with the stress of the approaching matriculation tests, which were looming huge on the horizon like a terrible mountain that needed to be scaled. She saw that she had to make some tough choices regarding her commitments and goals because her academic career was in threat. After she sat down, Elena's parents, Carla and Miguel, had a deep conversation about what would be best for Elena going forward. They discussed the benefits and drawbacks of her present extracurricular activities, taking into account how they might affect her general well-being and academic standing.

Elena knew something had to give, and after considerable thought, they decided that Elena's schoolwork would take precedence over her badminton love. Elena was sad about this choice. Elena had to say goodbye to her colleagues' friendship and the comfortable surroundings of the tennis classes, therefore it was a bittersweet occasion. However, despite the grief of saying goodbye to her friends, she found a glimmer of optimism and a feeling of purpose that drove her to continue on her path to academic success. Elena was resolved to make the most of this new chapter in her life, so she faced the challenges ahead with determination and resilience.

Elena made the choice and then cautiously stepped onto the new, foreign ground of her tuition lessons. She experienced a wave of unease when she was surrounded by strangers and faced difficult scholastic obstacles. She found it challenging to interact with her friends because of her introverted personality, and she had a hard time adjusting to this new atmosphere.

However, Elena saw that she was gradually emerging from her shell with every day that went by. Determined to make genuine relationships despite her initial fears, she cautiously smiled and struck up short conversations with her classmates. She was shocked to discover, too, that a large number of her students were happy to have her join them, showing her kindness and companionship in ways that made her feel comfortable.

Elena set off on a path of self-discovery and personal development as she threw herself into her studies and accepted the difficulties of her new academic endeavours. She devoted several hours to studying, reading through textbooks and attending intense study sessions in an effort to ace her matriculation tests and guarantee a successful future for herself.

Elena persevered in her goal despite the obstacles and disappointments that she would inevitably face. She began to rise to the demands of her scholastic obligations with fresh zeal and determination as each day went by, and her confidence continued to grow. This stage serves as a metaphor for Elena's tenacity and will in the face of difficulty as she makes her way through the foreign territory of her new tuition lessons. It demonstrates her steadfast dedication to accomplishing her objectives and emphasises the transformational potential of tenacity and self-belief in conquering life's challenges.

Elena was 18 already, and she had a lot of wild fantasies in her head. She was eager to experience all the things she had only read about in books and seen in films, including exploring her sexuality. She loved to envision herself in intimate, detailed fantasies with that one person. She had always been a committed person, so she found it exciting to consider exploring her desires with just one partner.

Being in control of her partner's life was one of Elena's greatest dreams. She would picture him muttering filthy things in her ear and telling her all he wanted to do to her, his breath hot on her skin. The sensation of his fingertips tracing every inch of her body made her heart accelerate. Elena dreamed of her boyfriend taking her clothes off carefully while appreciating each and every fold and curve on her body. He would tease and taunt her, leaving her desperate for his touch.

In her ideal world, Elena's partner would carefully undress her, appreciating each and every curve and crevice of her physique. She desired for her companion to adore and own every area of her body. In her dreams, she fully gave herself over to the man in charge, engaging in crude language and physical contact.

Elena's partner would ravish her and take advantage of her in every manner once he caved in. She would moan and groan beneath him as he used his lips and hands to explore every inch of her body. She cherished the sensation of total submission to her partner—of being totally taken over and dominated by him.

Sex in a romantic environment was one of Elena's other desires. As the waves smashed against the coast, she would picture herself and her partner lying in each other's arms on an isolated beach. With every caress and kiss, their passion would grow as they explored one other in the warm, soft sand under their bodies.

Elena also cherished the thought of being observed while having sex. She had an imaginary place where she and her lover lived in a penthouse with floor-to-ceiling windows that overlooked the city. As people on the street below observed, she would picture her lover giving her a gentle hug from behind and planting a kiss.

A variety of positions, each more thrilling and pleasurable than the previous, were also part of Elena's fantasies. She felt every inch of her companion filling her up, and she envisioned herself on top, riding him with wild passion. She also visualised being grabbed from behind, her lover claiming her, and the raw thrill of being mounted sending her into a frenzy of need.

She was determined to try every position, from the traditional missionary to the more daring ones like the reverse cowgirl or the standing wheelbarrow. The sensation of being entirely dependent on her lover, their bodies moving in perfect harmony as they descended into unprecedented levels of pleasure, was something she craved.

When her partner took her from behind, it was one of Elena's favourite positions in her fantasies. She cherished the sensation of her partner's hands squeezing her hips and drawing her towards him as she felt totally controlled and filled from behind. Elena would feel quite turned on in this position, but she would also feel exposed and vulnerable.

Elena also enjoyed fantasizing about making love in the shower. Her companion would push her against the chilly tiles while they probed each other's bodies in the warm, steamy water. Their passion would be even more intense when they felt the water rushing down their bodies, resulting in an even more thrilling encounter.

Deep in the darkest hours of the night, Elena treasured a silent yearning for her partner's soft touch among the seductive attraction of her wild and burning dreams. She found comfort in the simple act of lying in bed together, wrapped in each other's arms, their laughter and whispered secrets blending in the quiet, even beyond the thrill of daring meetings. She felt a deep sense of calm well up inside her at the notion of curling up with him and feeling his warm body against hers as they fell asleep.

Nothing held them back or demanded of them during those intimate hours under the cover of darkness—just their enduring love. She felt an unfathomable thrill that went beyond passion and need when she felt the gentle caress of his touch and the murmured promises of eternity. For Elena, the peaceful intimacy of such hugs had a captivating charm, a reminder of the strong connection that bound them in a world where time stood still and the beauty of their love was most radiant at night.

Elena's dreams were always changing and evolving, but her partner was something that never changed. She could not have imagined exploring her sexuality with anyone else, as he was the one who had brought all of her crazy dreams to life. Knowing that their love and desire would only deepen, she was looking forward to all the experiences and adventures they would have.

Finally, it can be said that Elena's dreams encompass a wide range of wants, from the passionate attraction of domination to the gentle closeness of passionate embraces. Her ideal relationship is the one that never changes, stoking her desires and providing the steadfast dedication needed to realize every aspect of her dreams. His presence brings deep fulfilment to every contact, whether it is in the peaceful embrace of calm times or the ferocious intensity of dominance. As they go through the limitless depths of desire, their connection acts as a lighthouse, guiding them. Together, they discover the depths of pleasure and intimacy. Beyond the confines of imagination and into the boundless potential of their journey together, Elena finds fulfilment in his embrace, along with the prospect of unending discovery and deep connection.

Amidst the relentless progression of time, Elena found herself settled into the busy hallways of her new tuition sessions, where every day presented a new chance for development and bonding. She was anxious to make her mark among a sea of fresh faces as she entered this strange world, mixed with a hint of optimism.

Elena's previously reserved manner started to soften as she made her way through the maze-like corridors of academia, opening out like a fragile flower in the early springtime. Day by day, she discovered that she was emerging from the shyness cocoon she had been wrapped in and embracing the colourful tapestry of human connection that these sacred halls held in store for her.

Elena was drawn to Lucas and Mia's magnetic presence among the cacophony of extracurricular activities and academic endeavours because they were a kind and genuine couple who shone like a lighthouse in the dark. Elena felt a connection to the two of them as soon as they met, their easy-going friendship and sincere love pulling her into their circle.

Elena rapidly grew to love Lucas' contagious laugh and boundless energy, his laid-back demeanour acting as a comfort to her restless spirit. Elena was captivated by Lucas's limitless energy and unshakable commitment, which made him a continual source of comfort as well as encouragement in her newfound path, whether they were having heated arguments or laughing together.

Mia, however, was the one who really won Elena over; something in her soul was ignited by her contagious energy and unrestrained enthusiasm. Elena was greeted by Mia with wide arms the instant they met, and her contagious laughter and sincere love woven a friendship fabric that would last. In the warmth of their shared company, Elena's concerns and doubts vanished, and she experienced a sense of belonging she had never had before with Mia at her side. They walked through the turbulent stages of growing up together, their relationship deepening with every day as they navigated through late-night talks and emotional admissions.

Elena discovered a kindred spirit in Mia, someone to share life's pleasures and tragedies with in addition to a confidante and companion. They were soul sisters connected by the bonds of love and loyalty because of their identical experiences and knowledge of one another, which went beyond simple friendship.

Day by day, the weeks stretched into months, and Elena really enjoyed the newfound friendship and camaraderie that Lucas and Mia had brought into her life. She handled the hardships of adulthood with courage and tenacity, knowing that she was never alone in her journey, thanks to their unfailing support and unconditional love.

This phase explores the complex fabric of friendship and emphasizes how human connection has the ability to change the world and have a significant influence on our lives. Through Elena's experiences, we see the relationships that are formed in the furnace of shared victories, tears, and laughter blossom, which is a monument to the human spirit's eternal power.

Mia and Elena were caught up in an open discussion during the tuition break. Mia chose to confide in Elena about her sexual orientation since she felt open and trusted with her. Mia took a deep breath and confessed to being bisexual—a secret she had kept from many people. As Mia talked more about her experiences, she revealed that she had gone further into her sexual exploration by going on a threesome with her boyfriend Lucas and best friend Alice. Mia waited to see how Elena would respond to the revelation, which hung in the air with a hint of weakness and a hint of release. He went on, though, because Elena was speechless and unsure of what to say.

Mia continued by saying that the decision for the threesome was motivated by their openness and shared interest. Being bisexual, Mia had freely declared her want to explore her desires, and Lucas, wanting to satisfy her as well as his own, had welcomed the idea with open arms.

With a playful sparkle in her eyes, Mia sat on the chair and started telling Elena about her experience of her threesome. "So, it all started with my boyfriend Lucas and my best friend Alice," she said, taking a long breath before speaking. Continuing the conversation, she said, "We had been friends for a long time and all of us were rather daring and open-minded when it came to having sex."

After a brief pause, she recalled that evening when she added, "We were all hanging out in my room, drinking and chatting. The talk eventually shifted to sexual topics as the evening wore on, and before we realized it, we were all making sexual jokes and getting excited about one other. I sensed the tension in the atmosphere and knew that something significant was going to occur."

Mia added after taking another long breath, "All of a sudden, Lucas leaned in and kissed me, and Alice did the same. We all three had our hands intertwined, roaming over each other's bodies while exchanging intense kisses. My pulse was thumping with anticipation as we started stripping off our clothes."

She went into great detail about how their hands went over each other's exposed parts as they undressed each other. Alice and Lucas alternated between kissing and grabbing her, their tongues and hands leaving a path of warm kisses and shivers down her spine.

As they were all naked, Mia let out a gasp when she felt Alice's lips wrap around her nipple, sucking and nibbling on it while Lucas whispered dirty words in her ear. She was immersed in the sensation, moaning and stretching her back.

Then, without any hurry or inhibitions, Mia described to Elena how they alternately enjoyed one other's company. "We forgot all of our boundaries and just let go because we were all so turned on and eager to please each other. A moment of pure joy and connection, it was beautiful and intense."

She spoke in graphic detail about how Alice lurched on top of Lucas as he gave Mia the finger and tongue pleasure. They then switched positions, Mia sucking on Alice's clit while Lucas entered her from behind. Every position they tried was more astonishing than the last as they carried on experimenting.

Mia moaned uncontrollably as she recalled what it was like to be pressed between Lucas and Alice, their bodies moving in perfect sync. Every touch and every sensation was amplified to the point of ecstasy—it was like being in a dream.

As the evening wore on, they experimented with various setups and positions repeatedly pushing one another to the limit of pleasure. Their only concern was the immense pleasure they were feeling, and they were completely lost in the moment.

Lastly, Mia talked about the explosive climax they all reached together. "As we all hit our climax together, we screamed and moaned in unison. We all passed out on the bed, sweating and panting from the sheer intensity and overpowering feeling of the release."

Mia added, "It was the most intense and mind-blowing experience of my life," as she turned to face Elena and met her gaze. "That night opened my eyes to a whole new level of pleasure and connection that I never would have imagined enjoying the company of both a man and a woman at the same time."

Breathless, Elena's thoughts were racing with the vivid pictures Mia's story had brought up. Mia smiled, knowing that she had given Elena a taste of the wild and pleasurable world she had experienced.

Following her disclosure of her experiences with threesome, Mia cautiously raised the idea of inviting Elena to take part in her and Lucas's private moments. But Mia was surprised by Elena's response. Elena said nothing, too shocked and uncomfortable to say anything. Elena remained silent in the face of Mia's optimistic question, but it was clear that she was uncomfortable and wouldn't consider the suggestion. Elena eventually found the confidence to say how she really felt, graciously turning down Mia's offer and clarifying her boundaries. Even though the exchange became difficult for a little while, Mia accepted Elena's choice since she understood how important it is for both parties to provide their agreement and understanding when it comes to private affairs.

Elena began to avoid Mia and Lucas as tuition was coming to an end. Her feelings were troubled by the awkward offer, which made her want to abandon their connection. Elena discreetly withdrew from the situation throughout the course of the previous month or two in an attempt to move on. She tried to appear normal, but the discomfort would not go away. Elena was more determined every day to keep her distance from Mia and Lucas in an effort to regain clarity and serenity in her life.

Chapter - 16
Embracing New Horizons

A new chapter in Elena's life started to take shape as the last few days of tuition were approaching and she passed her matric examinations for the 12th grade. With her sights set on going to college, she went off on a quest to see new places and pursue her aspirations of academic greatness.

Elena's dreams were driven by a desire to experience the freedom and independence that come with maturity, and they extended beyond the comfortable boundaries of her town. Having made up her mind to leave home in search of an education that would extend her boundaries and present her with fresh prospects, she boldly proposed her plan to her parents, Miguel and Alice.

Elena made it clear that she intended to pursue her studies outside of the comfortable boundaries of Soweto and Johannesburg. She was desperate for a new beginning, an opportunity to fly and forge her own way in the world. Miguel and Alice were first hesitant to listen to their daughter's passionate request. Still, they eventually saw how important it was to let her follow her aspirations at her own pace.

But even with her passion and determination, Elena's academic performance was insufficient to get her into some of the best engineering universities. Not to be defeated, Miguel used his contacts and influence to get in touch with an esteemed professor at the University of South Africa in Pretoria.

Elena's journey towards a university degree started to take form when she was offered a spot in the esteemed institution's bachelor's programme in computer science, thanks to Miguel's connections. Without her father's steadfast support and the influence of his connections, she would not have had such a wonderful chance.

For Elena, this was more than just a chance to pursue higher education – it was an opportunity to embrace new horizons, forge her own path, and become the architect of her own destiny. With determination in her heart and a thirst for knowledge in her soul, she eagerly embraced the challenges and possibilities that lay ahead, ready to embark on a transformative journey that would shape her future in ways she had never imagined.

Elena was excited and bursting with anticipation as she meticulously packed her belongings for her visit to Pretoria. A step closer to her goals of independence and academic success was symbolised by each item she folded and packed in her bag. She was excited about the prospect of taking on a journey that would alter her and about the prospect of experiencing new things. She was so excited about the possibility of experiencing the bustling campus life of the University of South Africa that her heart was racing as she carefully arranged her stuff. Elena was excited for the experiences that awaited her in Pretoria as she packed up each item. She was ready to meet new people, leave her past and her people behind, and take on new challenges.

Elena was eager to explore her academic interests and pursue her own path in life, so she set off on a voyage of self-discovery and intellectual study as soon as she was accepted. She was filled with excitement and expectation as she left behind the comfortable surroundings of home and arrived at the University of South Africa Campus.

Elena recognised that the path ahead would be difficult and full of hurdles, even as she looked forward to the future with hope and optimism. Nonetheless, she approached the uncertainty with bravery and resiliency, prepared to grab any chance that presented itself, thanks to the steadfast support of her family and the prospect of fresh starts. Her journey into maturity begins with this chapter, as she embarks on her quest for independence and a college degree. It's evidence of her fortitude, tenacity, and the value of family support in enduring change and seizing new chances.

As Elena entered the expansive campus of the University of South Africa in Pretoria, she could feel the excitement in her veins. She felt excited and full of possibilities because of the place's dynamic atmosphere, which seemed like the start of a new chapter in her life with every step she took. Her mind racing with enthusiasm for the experiences that awaited, she made her way to the hostel where she would be staying, her heart racing with excitement.

Upon settling into her cosy although compact space, Elena experienced a wave of freedom. The weight of her history did not restrain her from expressing herself fully here, in the privacy of her own place. She turned her room's walls into a canvas on which to paint her aspirations, each stroke serving as a symbol of her growing independence and determination.

In the days that followed, Elena discovered that she had to navigate the complexities of social contact while feeling both curious and nervous. She was a member of the tight-knit group of her classmates who were exchanging jokes, memes, and inside jokes on social media. She was hesitant at first to participate completely in their discussions, but she was comforted by watching from the sidelines, waiting to feel comfortable enough to do so.

Elena was hesitant at first, but she was eager to embrace the opportunities of the present and escape the confines of her history. She longed to establish deep bonds with her peers and produce enduring memories. She then set out into the world with a peaceful resolve, her heart open to whatever adventures awaited her.

After a demanding day of college, her friends made the decision to get together one evening at a neighbouring Italian restaurant to relax. Elena couldn't help but notice a tinge of fear eating away at her confidence as they took their seats. She was insecure about her habits and physical appearance, mindful of the impression she was making on her new friends.

Seated at the table, Elena observed her classmates laughing and chatting, their effortless companionship serving as a sharp reminder of her own persistent uneasiness. However, a classmate called Peter moved over and sat next to her, offering a friendly greeting that warmed her heart. Elena greeted his welcome with a nervous smile, appreciative of the chance to meet and get to know someone new.

Elena's eyes moved to the cigarette hanging from Peter's lips as they opened up a little conversation, a habit that seemed strange and unfamiliar to her. She was a little curious, but she quickly dismissed the idea of joining him, mindful of her own values and priorities. She silently promised herself at that very moment to be faithful to herself despite temptation.

Elena handled the complexities of social contact with a blend of confidence and elegance throughout the evening, her heart full of a quiet will to pave her own way. She confronted the uncertain path ahead with bravery and fortitude because she understood that every new experience offered a chance for development and change.

Elena had a wave of pride as she said goodbye to her classmates and headed back to her room. Even while she might not have completely integrated into her new social group just yet, she was aware that she was moving forward—one baby step at a time. The best was still to come, she realized as she fell asleep that night, her heart full of optimism for the future.

Elena's experience of accepting fresh starts and figuring out the complexities of social interaction as she starts her undergraduate career in Pretoria is captured in this chapter. It draws attention to her inner conflicts and her will to be loyal to herself regardless of social pressure to fit in and make new friends.

As Elena stepped inside the classroom, her eyes swept across the sea of people she didn't know, the day began with enthusiasm. As she sat down at a desk, she could feel the butterflies of joy dancing in her breasts mixed with a rush of anxious energy. Peter, the other student she had met the previous day, took up residence behind her, his familiarity providing a sense of security amidst the multitude of unfamiliar faces.

Peter greeted everyone politely and got to work, the quiet silence of the classroom broken only by the subtle click of his laptop's keys. Elena was captivated by his calm intensity and her curiosity was sparked by the mysterious atmosphere that enveloped him. She just watched him for a time, doubts and concerns racing through her head. Nevertheless, a timid grin appeared on her lips as she recognized his presence, a subtle sign of friendship in the face of uncertainty, despite the residual concerns that continued to cloud her mind.

With the lectures coming to a conclusion, Peter invited Elena to lunch, and her tentative grin was encouraged by his kind manner. She was hesitant at first, but her curiosity overcame her concerns and she found herself attracted by the idea of spending more time with him. But she declined, pointing to restaurant vouchers she had in an inept attempt to hide the glimmer of doubt that was pulling at her heart.

Peter got in touch with her again later in the day, suggesting that they go for a walk later that evening followed by dinner. The weight of her previous rejection weighed heavily on Elena as she hesitated, but in the end, her determination was strengthened by her renewed feeling of adventure, and she joined in. She was becoming more and more nervous as she went, but the thrill of the voyage kept her from feeling completely lost.

Elena came out of the apartment as twilight fell on the city, her heartbeat accelerating with excitement. As she joined him on the sidewalk, Peter waited politely, a warm smile brightening up his features. As they set off on their walk together, the calm streets echoed with the steady beat of their shoes. Elena was becoming more comfortable in Peter's company by the minute, their laughing and stories flowing between them like natural rhythms.

After their walk, they came to a busy gaming arcade where they enjoyed their mutual love of video games. Their favourite games engrossed them in their own universes where they laughed and competed, the worries of the outer world receding into the background. They spent hours basking in the straightforward happiness of friendship, their bond growing stronger with each passing moment.

As hunger began to rumble in their tummies, they decided to hunt for food and had dinner at a nearby restaurant. As they shared intimate details of their life with each other across the table, their laughing mingled with the sound of cutlery clattering and conversation. Elena found that she could open up to Peter and let go of her past wounds, despite the fact that it was difficult at first.

However, even in the warmth of their developing connection, Elena couldn't help but observe Peter's frequent use of cigarettes. This realization surprised her, but she decided to ignore it since she didn't want it to ruin the bond they were starting to build. Rather, she was appreciative of the company he provided and concentrated on the warmth and affection that surrounded them.

Elena felt a wave of satisfaction come over her as the evening came to an end and Peter walked her back to her room. She was aware that she was not alone, even though the road ahead was full of unknowns. She welcomed the unknown with every step, her heart full of excitement for the experiences that awaited her. That night, when she fell asleep, a tiny grin appeared on her lips. Her dreams were full of thoughts about the adventures and friendships that were still to come.

Embracing the uncertainties of the unknown with courage and curiosity, Elena overcomes the difficulties of establishing new relationships in an unfamiliar setting in this chapter. Even in the face of uncertainty, it demonstrates her readiness to venture outside of her comfort zone and learn new things.

As the days turned into weeks, Elena discovered that she looked forward to going on her walks with Peter, since each outing brought a feeling of excitement and companionship. With every day that went by, their friendship grew stronger thanks to their sincere chats and shared laughter. Even though it was unpleasant at first, they soon settled into a routine, their relationship growing warm from their common experiences.

They went on a variety of unplanned and different activities, from exciting escapades at the neighbourhood arcade to calm strolls around the city streets. Elena discovered that she was enjoying her independence and that the excitement of their adventures was lulling her worries. She had never felt so free as she did when Peter was at her side; his laid-back demeanour was a lighthouse in her darkest hours.

Their friendship penetrated every part of their life and went beyond their casual trips. Their mutual interest in academia strengthened their friendship as they attended lectures together. And even though they occasionally enjoyed the excitement of skipping class, their bond stayed strong, which is a measure of how close they were.

As they got to know each other better, rumours about their genuine connection started to spread among their friends. Some believed them to be a couple, pulled together by an unconscious attraction. Though they were confident that their relationship went beyond labels like these, Elena and Peter paid little to no attention to the rumours. All that separated them was a profound respect for one another and a passion for exploration that brought them together as two related souls.

When rumours about their friendship began to circulate, Elena and Peter did not let it affect them; their bond was stronger than any outside pressure. Despite rumours, they laughed because they knew their relationship was based on mutual respect and understanding.

In addition to this, nevertheless, Elena was struggling with strange feelings that were rising in her heart amid the jokes and friendship. Never before had she felt this strongly about anybody, and her feelings for Peter were becoming stronger every day. Her comfort came from his unfailing support and understanding, and she was charmed by his effortless charm and infectious enthusiasm.

Her anxiety, however, increased in sync with her growing affection for Peter. She had no idea where their friendship would go and didn't know how to handle each aspect of their developing connection. Still, she couldn't understand why she was pulled to him, her heart aching for the warmth of his company despite her fears.

A wave of warmth swept over Elena one evening as they strolled hand in hand through the busy downtown streets. She suddenly realised that her emotions for Peter went beyond simple mutual affection and went beyond friendship. She so badly wanted to show him her true feelings, to open up her heart and soul to him. She was unsure about his reaction to her confession, so she delayed.

Peter turned to face her, his mischievous eyes sparkling, as they concluded their walk. His voice was warm and kind as he said, "What do you think we grab some dinner?"

Elena experienced an upsurge of emotion that made her heart race in her chest. Her lips started to say something, but the words got stuck in her throat, lost in a sea of doubt. Rather, she nodded softly, staring into Peter's eyes with a depth of emotion that was evident.

As they strolled hand in hand in the direction of the closest restaurant, Elena couldn't help but wonder what was ahead for them. She was aware that their journey together was only getting started and that a flurry of exploration and adventure was ahead. Even though they didn't know what lay ahead, she found comfort in the idea that as long as they were together, they could withstand any storm.

Elena readied herself for the experiences that were ahead, anxious to explore the depths of her newfound sentiments and find out where the path would lead her. She was filled with excitement and eagerness.

This chapter dives into Elena and Peter's developing romance, examining the intricacies of their changing bond and the unpredictability that comes with falling in love. It acts as a moving reminder of the deep effect friendship can have on a person's heart and its transformational potential.

Chapter - 17
Shadows of the Past

As the days went by, Elena discovered that she and Peter were firmly committed to one another. In the blink of an eye, six months had passed, illustrating the passage of time with the memories they had weaved together. Their relationship, a fabric of understanding and common experiences became closer with every day that went by.

They had experienced a flurry of lectures, late-night study sessions, and spontaneous experiences throughout their first semester at college. They relied on one another for support and direction as they negotiated the difficulties of academics together. A source of stability in the face of uncertainty, their relationship had grown to be the foundation of their college experience.

They were sitting in the busy campus courtyard one day when Peter pointed out a girl who was walking by and commented on how she looked. Elena experienced a slight feeling of jealousy, but she ignored it since she didn't want to face the insecurity that was still there in her. Rather, she just kept quiet, staring at the floor.

With a laugh that echoed through the room, Peter laughed at her response and reached out to playfully pinch her cheek. Light-heartedly, he taunted, "Come on, Elena, don't tell me you're jealous."

His words caused her heart to skip a beat, causing a surge of warmth to flood through her body. With hesitation, she smiled at him, her mind wandering to a past era when her heart had belonged to someone else.

"Did you ever date anyone before?" With a questioning tone, Peter broke the ice between them.

After a brief period of hesitation, Elena hesitantly nodded. Her eyes strayed to the horizon as she said, "Yes, I did. However, things didn't work out nicely. It still stung even after we both decided to part ways."

As Peter heard what she had to say, his countenance became more sympathetic. With grief in his voice, he replied quietly, "I'm sorry to hear that. Love can be complicated sometimes, huh?"

With a sad smile pulling at the outer edges of her lips, Elena nodded in mutual agreement. She said, "Yeah, it definitely can be," as her mind wandered to Jake and the tragic end of their love.

Peter also disclosed that he had dated three other women in the past, but that his most recent ex-girlfriend had been quite toxic and had ultimately damaged him. Elena expressed her sympathy for Jake's experiences and listened intently as he talked about his challenges. Despite his challenges, Jake understood the need to identify harmful connections and put his own health first.

Peter's arms wrapped around her in a show of friendship and support, and his expression softened as he reached out to give her a consoling embrace. A tribute to the strength of their love, it was a simple hug full of silent understanding and unsaid words.

Elena experienced a wave of calm as they stood wrapped in one other's arms at that very time. She was aware that she was not alone, even in the face of the heartbreaks from the past and the uncertainty of the future. She had finally met a buddy who understood her shortcomings and praised her talents.

As they parted ways, Elena couldn't help but feel a surge of gratitude for the friendship they shared. In Peter, she had found a confidant, a companion, and a source of unwavering support. And as they continued on their journey through college and beyond, she knew that their bond would only grow stronger with time.

This chapter delves into the evolving dynamics of Elena and Peter's friendship, exploring the complexities of their past relationships and the unbreakable bond that binds them together. It serves as a poignant reminder of the healing power of friendship and the importance of having someone to lean on in times of need.

As the whispers of their friendship echoed through the campus corridors, Elena and Jake found themselves unwittingly thrust into the spotlight. Even though their friendship was platonic, it attracted the interest of their classmates and sparked rumours. Elena and Jake's relationship remained unwavering in the face of the circulating rumours, despite the increasing talk surrounding them.

Elena found herself stepping outside of her close-knit group as she became more and more eager to completely immerse herself in college life. She spoke with others on anything from academic endeavours to events occurring on campus, her kind disposition encouraging others to join her. She made friends with a wide range of individuals in the midst of the busy hallways and colourful conversations, each interaction enhancing her college experience.

However, among the joy of making new acquaintances, Elena came upon a worrisome realization. One afternoon, a bunch of girls walked up to her, their faces slightly uncomfortable. They told Peter about their experiences in a timid voice before he got near to Elena. They talked of strange experiences, saying that Peter had been too eager to get close to them, that his motivations were unclear, and that his manner was uncomfortable.

Elena's view of her friendship with Peter was clouded by the weight of their words, which hung heavily in the air. She found it difficult to balance the disturbing charges made by these females with the impression of her reliable buddy. Her conscience was plagued by doubt, which threatened to break the ties that bound her.

Peter, anxious in his expression, stepped closer to Elena as he sensed her discomfort. His eyes were full of real concern as he asked her softly whether she was okay. Elena spoke hesitantly about the unsettling experience, her words filled with fear and fear. With a concerned expression on his face, Peter paid close attention, taking in the serious implications of her disclosure.

Peter's voice was firm and comforting when he spoke after a period of thoughtful stillness. He sympathised with Elena's worries and expressed his own shock at the charges made against him. He told Elena, with all seriousness, that he would always be there for her as a friend, stressing the strength of their relationship and the mutual trust.

In a touching conversation, Peter advised Elena not to allow other people's remarks to undermine their connection. He emphasised the value of understanding and trust while reaffirming his dedication to their common path. Elena was moved by his remarks and experienced a rush of relief as the comforting certainty of Peter lifted the weight of her uncertainties.

During their evening together, Peter broached a topic of trust, asking Elena whom she trusted more – him or the other girls. The question caught Elena off guard, and she paused before hesitantly acknowledging that she trusted Peter more than the other girls. Taking advantage of the moment, Peter warned Elena not to let anybody else step in or have any influence on their relationship and pushed her to protect their love with tremendous determination. He told Elena that it was crucial to keep their relationship going and that she should not interact with the other girls going forward.

Elena found inspiration in Peter's remarks, and she became determined to guard their developing relationship. As they said their goodbyes for the evening, Elena began to think back on Peter's advice and realized how important it was to protect their connection from outside influences. Elena felt a sudden feeling of commitment to put their link above all else and resolved to manage the complexity of their relationship with care and devotion, even if she wasn't sure what Peter's warning meant.

Their bond was reinforced as they strolled hand in hand. They developed a kinship in the furnace of hardship and confronted the challenges that lay ahead together. Elena discovered in Peter not just a companion but also a reliable comrade, a ray of hope and comprehension in an unpredictable world.

This chapter delves into the complexities of trust and loyalty as Elena and Peter navigate a challenging situation. Their friendship, which is based on openness, compassion, and steadfast support, is highlighted by this. Their relationship is unshakeable in the face of hardship as they endure uncertainties and suspicions together and come out stronger.

As the semester came to an end and examinations loomed like storm clouds gathering far in the distance, Elena could not help but think about Peter's sincere question as it resonated through her mind's corridors of thought. She was filled with a whirlwind of feelings that whirled about her like leaves caught in the wind at the thought of going on a romantic adventure with Peter. Elena was surrounded by warmth and comfort in Peter's company, but she was also caught in a maze of uncertainty and doubt, her heart divided between the need for company and the fear of experiencing the same painful experiences again.

Elena found solace in the isolation of her thoughts during the hectic rush of late-night study sessions and last-minute cramming, struggling with the important choice that was in front of her like an immovable boulder obstructing her way. Every day that went by was a new wave of uncertainty that threatened to submerge her in a sea of uncertainty and fear. Still, in the middle of the flurry of approaching tests and approaching deadlines, the question hung there like a recurring theme, pleading for her consideration.

Elena found herself in an uncertain circumstance where she had to make a decision that may drastically change her life as the semester came to an end and the prospect of the holiday season became closer. In the comfortable embrace of her family and friends, in the warmth of her Soweto homeland, she struggled with the impossible task of letting love into her heart again. Elena navigated the turbulent seas of her deepest thoughts and feelings, experiencing a kaleidoscope of emotions with each passing second, from excitement to anxiety.

During quiet times of reflection, Elena permitted herself to consider the prospect of a future with Peter. She pictured a tapestry filled with whispered promises and shared dreams. Even with the scars from past heartbreaks still visible, she understood that genuine courage was about accepting change and letting go of her fear of opening her heart to another person. Elena decided to take a risk and say yes to Peter's sincere request, her steely resolve stemming from her newfound resolve.

With the magic of modern equipment, Elena and Peter were able to connect during the peaceful days of the vacation season, when Soweto was bathed in the golden light of the sun and Durban shimmered beneath the blue expanse of the sky. The warm glow of screens illuminated their faces as they laughed and conversed across the distances, and the quiet chime of video call alerts interspersed their days. They remained on video chats from the crack of morning till the quiet murmurs of midnight, their voices a calming symphony that reverberated through the ether, creating a tapestry of connection that broke down barriers of time and location. Their emotions intertwined in a dance of whispered vows and shared dreams, they found comfort in one other's company during those few moments spent together.

Elena felt a mixture of excitement and anxiety as the semester drew to an end and the holiday period approached, her pulse racing at the thought of fresh starts. Split apart by the vastness of South Africa, Elena lived in Soweto and Peter in Durban; they looked forward to seeing each other again after the semester break. With optimism and the promise of a better tomorrow in their hearts, they started a new chapter in their lives together.

Elena's choice to accept the unpredictability of the future and risk falling in love with Peter marks the chapter's conclusion. She musters the bravery to accept his proposal despite her reservations and painful history, realising that it represents a fresh start and a leap of faith into the uncharted.

Elena and Peter find comfort in one other's company as they work through the difficulties of a long-distance relationship throughout the holidays, and their connection gets closer every day. They set forth on a path full of promise and opportunity, prepared to confront any obstacles that may arise as a team, with optimism and hope in their hearts.

Chapter - 18
Elena's Journey Through the Pandemic Storm

Elena was caught up in the turmoil of a worldwide crisis as the holiday season approached, promising rest and happiness. Even the quietest nooks of her Soweto neighbourhood were hit by the COVID-19 pandemic news, which spread like wildfire. With its origins in Wuhan, China, the virus soon gained widespread recognition and cast a pall over the whole world.

The epidemic caused Elena to experience a wide range of emotions as she considered the ramifications of this unheard-of calamity. She couldn't help but feel a feeling of anxiety and apprehension seeping into her heart as she watched the news broadcasts documenting the virus's rapid spread and the growing death toll. What would this entail for her future, her loved ones, and herself?

It was soon hard to deny the pandemic's effects as South Africa, like many other countries, had to deal with its full impact. Amidst the surge in cases, hospitals were overcrowded and medical supplies were nearly depleted, causing strain on the healthcare system. The idea of the virus entering their life worried Elena much because her family had already had enough health issues.

Following the epidemic, South Africa experienced economic instability as lockdown measures caused firms to cease operations and resulted in a large number of unemployed people. During the chaos, there was an increase in poverty and hunger, which made already existent disparities worse and made it difficult for vulnerable people to get food and other essentials. The epidemic made social problems—like gender-based violence and mental health disorders—worse, adding to the load being placed on already troubled communities. The necessity for fair access to vaccinations was highlighted by obstacles encountered throughout the vaccine rollout, such as supply chain problems and vaccine reluctance.

Elena observed her friends and neighbours fighting to make ends meet while facing threats to their livelihoods from uncontrollable circumstances. The formerly busy streets of Soweto were shrouded in a veil of anxiety about the future. Elena discovered herself battling the psychological and social effects of loneliness and uncertainty as the epidemic continued. Closures of colleges and schools interfered with her education and left her feeling lost and alone in an unknown world. A feeling of anxiety and disquiet took the place of the once-familiar routines of everyday life as she dealt with the difficulties of social separation and distant learning.

Despite the difficulties, Elena took comfort in her neighbourhood's resiliency, as neighbours banded together to help one another through hardship. They discovered methods for staying in touch and supporting one another during these difficult circumstances, such as food drives and online get-togethers. Elena knew that they would weather the storm together and come out stronger on the other side, so she never gave up hope.

Elena's determination was put to the test more than ever as the epidemic progressed. She was, however, unwavering in her resolve to face hardship head-on and come out stronger on the other side. Elena also saw that when things started to gradually get better, she had more hope and optimism for the future since she and her partner had survived the storm and come out stronger on the other side.

Elena was forced to navigate a turbulent terrain from the safety of her house as the COVID-19 epidemic spread with previously unheard-of speed and scope, enveloping the whole planet in a state of fear and confusion. With universities suddenly shuttering and tight lockdowns enforced, society was thrust into unknown terrain, forcing people to face a multitude of difficulties while trying to find comfort in the midst of it all.

Elena, like with many others, had to develop a deep degree of flexibility and resilience in order to adjust to the new reality. Elena discovered that new and creative ways to maintain relationships with friends and family were welcome after the disruption of conventional means of social connection. She learned how technology can overcome physical distance and create a feeling of community even in remote locations through virtual get-togethers and online forums.

However, Elena found herself struggling with the impact that extended social isolation and uncertainty were putting on her mental health as the days turned into weeks and the weeks into months. She was feeling overwhelmed and nervous because of the constant barrage of upsetting news and the lack of social ties and old routines. Elena understood how important it was to put herself first and worked hard to develop habits that supported her mental and emotional well, whether they were artistic endeavours, mindfulness exercises, or asking for help from loved ones.

A sobering reminder of humanity's interdependence with the environment was provided by the pandemic when lockdown measures resulted in a brief decrease in carbon emissions and air pollution. This gave Elena a serious wake-up call about the pressing need for sustainable habits and group action to solve the climate problem. Elena decided the decision to contribute to the development of a more just and sustainable future for future generations after seeing the contrast between the natural world's fragility and the human spirit's resiliency.

But in the middle of all the chaos and uncertainty, there were also times of optimism and unity when people banded together to help one another out with acts of generosity and compassion. Elena was able to see firsthand the strength of human fortitude and solidarity as neighbours banded together to support those in need, first responders bravely remained on the front lines of the crisis, and people from all walks of life discovered that they could draw strength from one another when faced with hardship.

Elena discovered that she was getting strength from her family as the pandemic progressed and that she treasured the times when they were able to spend time together and connect despite everything. Amidst a constantly shifting environment, the moments she spent playing cards with her father Miguel, laughing with her brother Diego, watching films with her family, and finding comfort in the arms of her loved ones served as anchors of stability.

Elena turned to online platforms, especially social media and online games, for comfort and connection during the difficult moments of the epidemic. She and Peter were separated by physical distance, but they remained connected virtually, spending many hours conversing and playing games on social media. They were able to overcome the distance caused by the epidemic through these virtual exchanges, finding solace and camaraderie in one other's virtual company. Their internet connection was a lifeline, giving them moments of happiness and connection in the middle of the upheaval of the outside world as they negotiated the uncertainties of the crisis. And with it all, her relationship with Peter became closer as they provided comfort and support to one another in the midst of uncertainty.

In the end, Elena emerged from the epidemic with a fresh understanding of the human spirit's resiliency and the strength of the community during difficult times as society gradually started to recover. She confronted the future with bravery and resolve, prepared to seize whatever possibilities and challenges awaited, even while the path ahead remained undetermined.

Elena and Peter found themselves setting off on a trip that would put their love to the test like never before against the backdrop of a world struggling with the extraordinary problems brought forth by the epidemic. Colleges closing and strict physical distance regulations imposed on them meant that they had no choice but to rely on the internet to stay in touch, creating a relationship that went beyond physical proximity.

Elena tucked herself into the virtual world that linked her and Peter in the comfort of her own room, lit by the gentle glow of her laptop. A source of consolation and comfort in the face of uncertainty, their nightly video conversations became indispensable. Every talk they had was evidence of the depth of their relationship as they laughed together, told each other stories about their days, and ventured into their souls.

Their minds danced together in a ballet of love and need, their hearts beating in time despite the distance between them. They delighted in the little joys of being virtually together, even in the banal activities of cooking dinner together, watching movies together, and having late-night talks that lasted well into the morning. A fragment of their hearts was embedded in every pixelated picture on the screen, serving as a constant reminder of the love that kept them connected despite their physical separation.

With grace and perseverance, Elena and Peter managed the ups and downs of their love as days moved into weeks and weeks into months. They supported and encouraged each other without hesitation at difficult moments as they navigated the unpredictability of life. They were able to navigate the turbulent waters of loneliness and isolation due to their virtual connection, which acted as a lifeline and a light of hope in the dark.

In spite of this, a sense of desire persisted in the warmth of their virtual embrace—a yearning for the day when they might be together in person for the very first time. When they held each other close, felt the warmth of their touch, and whispered love words into the darkness, it was the moment they dreamt of. They took comfort, however, in the fact that their love was unbounded and did not respect time or geography for the time being.

Peter made a choice that altered the nature of their relationship as the epidemic continued to affect their lives. They were talking on a video chat one evening when Peter reluctantly said he had chosen to transfer to a college in Durban, his birthplace. He described how studying near his family would provide him with more comfort and security because he felt that being so far away from home in such an uncertain period was wearing him down.

Elena experienced a rush of emotions as the weight of Peter's choice descended on her. Seated in her darkened room, her anxious expression illuminated by the illumination from her laptop, she went over their talk over and over in her head, picking apart every word he had said. She was caught off guard by the news, which left her feeling vulnerable and lost. It was like a sudden storm.

Just the word Durban evoked thoughts of far-off coasts and strange perspectives. The busy Pretoria campus and the well-known neighbourhoods of Soweto seemed a world apart. There was a hollowness in her that seemed to come from the notion of Peter being so far away, as if something had suddenly parted from her. The idea of managing a distant relationship during a pandemic appeared extremely difficult and intimidating, like a massive obstacle that was far ahead of them.

But even in the middle of her emotional turbulence, Elena saw a glimmer of resolve blazing within her. She was not going to allow doubt and anxiety to dominate their relationship. She promised to stick by Peter's side no matter how far apart they were from one another, with a resolution that came from love and courage. They had conquered challenges in the past, and she was resolved to take on this new one.

They did not make the choice to undertake a long-distance romance lightly. It was an oath—a pledge to one another to endure hardship and to foster their relationship in spite of the distance in kilometres that separated them. They were prepared to battle for their love, to overcome the obstacles, and to come out stronger on the other side even though they knew it wouldn't be simple.

Elena and Peter took comfort in the fact that they were not alone as they said goodnight to one another that night, their hearts heaving at the weight of their choice. Their love would be a guiding light through the darkest of nights as they navigated the unknown seas that lay ahead of them together. As they fell asleep, Elena felt at ease because she knew that she would face the future with Peter at her side, no matter what it brought.

Elena and Peter stuck to their commitment to one another even as the globe gradually started to come out of the pandemic's shadow. They were aware that their adventure was only getting started and that they still had a lot of difficulties ahead of them. But with love as their beacon, they accepted their separation, knowing that their hearts would always beat as one regardless of how far away they were.

Chapter - 19
Shadows of Doubt

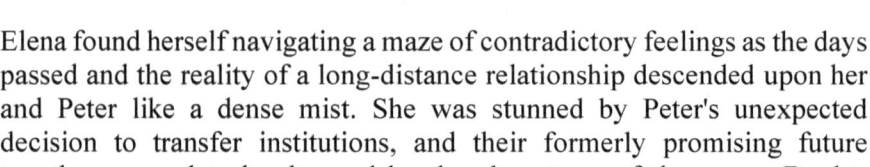

Elena found herself navigating a maze of contradictory feelings as the days passed and the reality of a long-distance relationship descended upon her and Peter like a dense mist. She was stunned by Peter's unexpected decision to transfer institutions, and their formerly promising future together seemed to be doomed by the abruptness of the move. Doubts slowly seeped into Elena's consciousness with every second that went by, posing a threat to the delicate bonds that held their hearts together.

Elena felt as if she was adrift in a sea of uncertainty when she learned of Peter's decision to switch colleges. The news was like a sledgehammer to her soul. She struggled with a flurry of opposing feelings, caught between the need to cling to their affection and the anxiety of what may come. She was plagued by doubts about their once-unwavering relationship as the idea of being separated by miles seemed to hang over her like a gloomy cloud.

Elena found herself thinking back on past choices with remorse and reflection following Peter's college transfer and the intimidating possibility of a long-distance relationship hanging over her. She thought back to a past relationship she had with Jake that had failed due to the difficulties of distance, a choice she had since grown to regret.

Elena decided to fight for her relationship with Peter and to face the obstacles head-on, determined not to make the same mistake twice. She would not let the ghost of distance cloud their love. She embraced the chance to build a future full of love and possibilities and gave her all to their journey together, taking courage from her past experiences and resolving to never give up. She swore to fight for her relationship with Peter despite all the challenges they encountered, determined not to make the same errors again.

Elena decided to commit to their relationship, bringing strength from their shared love and their shared experiences, despite having a heavy heart and a strong spirit. She brought herself back to the giggles that had filled the hallways as they relived their past encounters, the happy moments that had brightened even the worst of days. She desperately hoped that their love would last the storm and come out stronger on the other side, even in the face of all the uncertainty that was ahead.

Elena sent meaningful birthday gifts to Peter as a way of demonstrating her dedication to their relationship. She put her all into every gift in an attempt to show how much she loved and cared about the recipient. She had no idea that the sincere actions she took would unintentionally reveal a terrible reality that was lying under the surface.

Elena and Peter had a connection that went beyond just talking and being in person; they shared a digital space where memories were treasured and kept safe. Their shared cloud storage acted as a digital file cabinet for their photos, a virtual archive of their times together caught in pixels. Every picture, whether they were silly selfies, recollections of important events, or snippets from their trips together, told a tale and demonstrated how deeply they were connected. Because the disc was so open, they could access every photo and memory, which encouraged openness and intimacy in their relationship. Their love transcended the physical distance that frequently divided them in this digital world, finding expression in pixels and bytes.

Elena's heart fluttered with anticipation as Peter's birthday drew near and she watched to see how he responded to her presents. She soon discovered a startling realisation, though, as her exhilaration quickly gave way to agony. As Elena browsed through their shared cloud storage, she came upon pictures of Peter's birthday celebration with his ex-girlfriend. Elena saw the pictures the instant they were captured and stored, but she became even more concerned when she saw that suspicious pictures of Peter and his ex-girlfriend had been quickly removed from the storage just a few hours after they had been taken.

Elena felt as if a lightning bolt had hit when she saw Peter hugging his ex in front of an extravagant bouquet of flowers. Betrayal struck with a swift, sharp pain that sliced through her heart like a hot knife. She recognised how cruel Peter's actions had been, and tears filled her eyes as she tried to make sense of the picture of the man she loved and the dreadful truth that was now before her. Despite Peter's previous assertions that his ex-girlfriend was toxic and that he hadn't been in contact with her for the past six months, Elena's discovery of the photos together, on his birthday painted a starkly different picture, leading her to question the truthfulness of his statements.

Elena had a moment of agony and despair when it felt like everything was falling apart around her, completely upending the basis of her relationship. She was overcome with a flurry of contradictory feelings, alternating between despair, indignation, and a deep feeling of betrayal. She felt lost and alone in a large sea of doubt as a result of Peter's dishonesty, which tore at her soul.

Elena deliberately chose not to approach Peter about the images she had seen, even with shock and conflict whirling around her. Rather, she opted to preserve the impression of normalcy on the outside while concealing her inside struggle with a calm exterior. She played the character of the gullible girlfriend with a heavy heart, carrying on their regular exchanges and discussions as though nothing had changed. However, her mind was filled with uncertainties and concerns underneath the surface, and every silent moment they shared was charged with unsaid anxiety. Elena appeared to be at ease, but below she was determined to keep a tight eye on Peter's actions and to look for any indications of dishonesty or treachery that would allay her darkest suspicions.

Elena couldn't help but question whether their love was strong enough to weather the storm that was about to blow them apart. In the middle of her suffering, she clung to the sliver of hope that was still present in her heart and prayed for a glimpse of knowledge and salvation. However, she secretly worried that the information she had discovered would destroy their relationship forever, leaving nothing but broken promises and crushed hopes in its wake.

After learning of the disturbing revelation, Elena was thrown into a turbulent tornado of feelings, each stronger than the last. The pictures stuck in her head, clear and sharp, as if to mock her with their indisputable proof of Peter's alleged treachery. Elena chose not to tell Peter what she had discovered, even though she was tormented within. Instead of approaching him right away, she decided to confirm that her suspicions were valid. She loved him and didn't want to part with him, so she was always praying that her suspicions weren't true.

Days stretched into nights, and Elena found it difficult to keep things somewhat normal while she was with Peter. Notwithstanding her calm exterior, her thoughts were constantly racing with a plethora of queries and uncertainties, all of which were nibbling at the edges of her awareness. Through a maze of lies, she examined every word and move Peter made, looking for any hint of the truth. In addition, Peter had not previously disclosed to Elena that his ex-girlfriend was a student at the same university to which he had just relocated.

Elena felt a strong wave of intuition take hold of her while she and Peter were talking aimlessly on the phone late one fateful night. A few seconds after saying goodbye to Peter, Elena gave in to the overwhelming impulse to contact him, despite the slight quiver of anxiety coursing through her veins. It was a far cry from the smooth connection they'd had minutes before when the phone rang nonstop and all she got was a constant busy signal, much to her distress.

Elena struggled to understand the consequences of Peter's unexpected absence, her confusion mixed with shock. She could not stop thinking about all the terrifying possibilities that flashed through her thoughts. Elena was sceptical, though, because worries persisted at the back of her mind like shadows thrown by a ghostly presence even when Peter had answered her call.

Elena was at first unconcerned by Peter's explanation and took his word for the phone interruption. She took comfort in Peter's quick screenshot of the contact stored under her brother's name, believing him when he said her brother needed to unlock the gate. However, there was a small question that continued to bother her subconscious—a gnawing uncertainty about the unexpected phone call. Elena's interest was aroused even though she immediately wrote it off, considering it a small annoyance. Not wanting to let go of the lingering sense of discomfort, she went back to the screenshot the next day and examined it with a renewed sense of purpose.

Elena's concerns were confirmed when she looked more closely and saw a little trace beneath her brother's touch, an unimportant detail that might shatter the illusion of confidence. She was reluctant to look into it more at first, but curiosity drove her to do so. She traced the hidden digits with quivering fingers as a feeling of dread settled in the pit of her stomach.

There was a twinge of anxiety in her when she entered the coded number into her phone. She was waiting for the result, breathless, her heart racing. The phone continued to ring, marking the passage of time as if it were a sign of something more to come. The call connected, and the chime that always signals the beginning of an unchangeable journey towards truth, sounded as if it were meant to.

That thin layer of trust was destroyed as the voice on the other phone verified her darkest suspicions. It was a terrifying confirmation of treachery. With the utter stillness of her empty room around her, Elena experienced the burden of dishonesty at that very moment. She shed a lot of tears as she dealt with the painful truth of Peter's duplicity, a wave of emotions rushing through her. With such heartbreaking information, she felt alone and overwhelmed, sinking to the floor and being overcome by a whirlwind of contradictory feelings as she considered what to do next.

The weight of treachery tore Elena's heart apart as she withdrew into the comfort of her chamber, overwhelmed by a whirlwind of rival feelings. Her thoughts were absorbed by the terrifying idea of approaching Peter with the incriminating proof she had unearthed, as shown by the silent tears that streamed down her face.

Later on in the day, Elena sought consolation from her friends as she was still in shock from the events that had transpired. She went out to others who had previously expressed doubts about Peter's character, desperate for advice and encouragement. She told him about the disturbing revelation of Peter's duplicity on his birthday and the subsequent disclosure of his ex-girlfriend's participation, all with a sad heart.

Her friends listened with wide eyes that reflected the mix of shock and confusion that Elena was feeling herself. Although they had a suspicion that Peter was dishonest, they were equally shocked by how far he had gone with his lie. They united around Elena, providing her with steadfast support and solidarity during her time of need. They were determined to find the truth and tackle the treachery head-on.

They came up with a strategy to go up against the person who was behind the fraud, the enigmatic number that had raised questions about Elena and Peter's relationship. They dialled the number with a mixture of fear and resolve, each ringing like a loud cry for justice and resolution.

There was a tangible sense of expectancy and tension when the phone connected. Elena asked the question that had been bothering her ever since she found out about Peter's deception in a steady voice. "Who's Peter to you?" she asked, fear racing through her body.

First, there was hesitancy, a long, breathless silence that seemed to go on forever. Finally, there was an answer, an acknowledgement that tore apart Peter's fragile mask of innocence. The person on the other end of the call admitted that Peter was actually her boyfriend. Elena was struck hard by the realisation, which brought home the terrible truth of Peter's treachery.

Elena and the girl formed an improbable bond during that exchange of understanding, connected only by the agonising reality of Peter's deceit. A spirit of camaraderie that offered a ray of hope amidst the rubble of broken trust passed between them as they commiserated over their common experiences and traded stories. They pledged to confront Peter and reveal his falsehoods as a group, unified in their quest for justice and closure.

After that phone call, Elena forced herself to address Peter about the devastating information that had come to light, despite having a heavy heart and a knot of anxiousness in her stomach. Her voice was shaking with a mix of hurt, fury, and bewilderment as she related what had happened that day. The thin threads of trust that had once kept their relationship intact were being threatened by Peter's betrayal, and the weight of it all weighed heavily on her with every word.

Elena kept a close eye on Peter's face as the truth came to light, looking for any indication of regret or shame. Rather than feeling regret, however, she was confronted with an astonishing realisation: Peter had been managing two relationships at the same time, conjuring up a web of lies much more complex than she could have ever imagined. While Elena struggled to process the shock and anguish of his betrayal, his attempts at explanation were met with silence.

Peter made explanations and reasons, assigning blame and pointing fingers in an attempt to minimise his own responsibility, all in a desperate attempt to save what was left of their relationship. A weak apology and a limp attempt at healing were all he offered Elena, but the harm had already been done, their once-loved relationship permanently damaged.

Listening to Peter try to place the blame on her, to paint her as the mastermind behind their demise, Elena felt hopeless and defeated. He accused her of speeding their death with her impatience and insistence on the truth, a charge that stung deeply and reopened wounds that had just started to heal.

"If only you had waited two more days," Peter complained, his voice tinged with bitterness and frustration, "this wouldn't have happened. I was about to break up with her"

Peter's words struck a deep chord with Elena, a harsh turn of events that left her reeling from a deep sense of betrayal. Their already damaged relationship was further strained by the weight of his accusation, which hung heavily in the air. Elena, however, remained unwavering in the face of chaos and would not accept Peter's attempts to place the responsibility on her.

Elena, her heart heavy and tears in her eyes, knew that she could not take Peter's dishonesty and falsehoods any longer. Her choice to leave Peter and the unhealthy relationship that had trapped her for far too long came to her in that flash of clarity. Her next words were, "It's over, Peter", something she never imagined she would say, "I'm worthy of better."

Elena had no idea that the complex emotional web that connected her to Peter had ensnared her even in the midst of the pain and betrayal. Peter's silver tongue worked its charm repeatedly, tying Elena's heartstrings with a tapestry of apologies and promises. Time and again, Elena found herself giving in to his demands, her feelings for him impairing her sense of reason and overwhelming her better judgment. Even with all of the suffering and anguish, Elena held onto the little hope that their relationship may still be saved. Against her better judgement, she chose to stay, as her heart yearned for the love and affection that Peter had previously assured her of.

Elena was left feeling conflicted over the treachery she had just learned about and the love she still had for Peter following their fight and his confession. Peter told her how sorry he was, that it had all been an error in judgement, and he begged her forgiveness as he spoke. While concerns persisted, Elena couldn't help but sense a glimmer of optimism that they could get through this together because of his words, which were like a salve to her hurting heart.

Peter did, however, set forth terms for their reunion in addition to his apology. He told Elena that he was afraid of outsiders getting involved in their relationship and pleaded with her not to. Worried that her college acquaintances may turn her against him, he brought up her classmates in particular. In addition, Peter asked Elena to cut off her connection with his ex-girlfriend and to avoid becoming too close to the other females who had tried to warn her about him.

Elena hesitantly agreed assuming that by doing so, she would be able to save their relationship despite the severity of his demands. Even though she knew in her heart that forgiveness wouldn't make the hurt of betrayal go away, her continued love for Peter forced her to give him another opportunity, even if it meant treading carefully.

Chapter - 20
Fragile Trust

Beneath the surface, the betrayal scars continued to fester, ready to burst at any time while Elena and Peter cautiously resumed their relationship. In the middle of uncertainty and uneasiness, Elena's love for Peter remained a ray of hope, holding her heart close to him. However, the consequences of his previous wrongdoings continued to put a fog over their newly discovered pleasure and their interactions with one another.

Elena was experiencing intense emotions that were at odds with each other as she tried to mend the broken trust. Even though she desperately wanted to trust that Peter was sincere and that he had kept his word, the ghost of his past lingered in her memory, following her about at all times. Doubts gnawed at Elena's heart like a merciless beast, threatening to devour her frail hopes with every day that passed, despite his extensive apologies and promises.

Elena frequently found herself looking to Peter for comfort and assurance, requesting texts and screenshots as evidence of his faithfulness in an attempt to calm her anxieties and stem the flow of suspicion. Even though Peter obeyed, their relationship was stressed by his incessant need for affirmation, which made even the most routine conversations into fraught situations involving distrust and insecurity. Their talks, which had previously been easy-going, were now tense and burdened down by their pasts with every word.

Peter saw Elena's relentless requests for evidence as a harsh critique of his previous mistakes and an ongoing reminder of his failure to live up to the confidence she had put in him. Peter was frustrated that Elena couldn't let go of his previous mistakes, and he found it difficult to fully understand her remaining doubts. His attempts to reassure her were received with negativity and disbelief.

As they negotiated the perilous terrain of trust and betrayal, their relationship evolved into a delicate ballet of push and pull that stood on the edge of doubt. Their love and dedication to one another were put to the test as each day presented fresh difficulties and barriers. But even in the middle of all the confusion and uncertainty, there was a glimmer of hope—a flickering flame that defied the darkness that tried to swallow them up.

Days became weeks, and weeks became months, as Elena and Peter were stuck trying to put what had been destroyed back together nonstop. In the face of uncertainty, their love for one another provided consolation and comfort, acting as a guiding light in the dark. However, there was still a long way to go and a lot of danger ahead, a narrow path with many of hazards that might easily throw their tenuous peace off course.

Elena and Peter persevered in their love for one another despite the difficulties they encountered and resolved to get through the difficulties their future held. As their love acted as a lighthouse of hope in the midst of the night, they found the strength to withstand the storms that raged around them in each other's arms. A monument to the lasting strength of love in the face of difficulty, their link remained unbroken even if their trust was brittle.

Elena was caught in a maelstrom of contradictory feelings as the day of her departure approached. She was excited and nervous at the same time about going back to college after more than a year of online education. She was excited to see her friends again and enjoy being a part of the campus scene, the spirit of Peter's presence in Durban loomed large in her mind, casting a shadow of doubt over her newfound sense of freedom.

When the government decided to partly reopen schools and universities after students like Elena endured nearly a year of online lessons due to the COVID-19 outbreak, it was a mixture of relief and fear. Many people still had worries about the growing epidemic, even if the idea of going back to school provided some sort of normalcy after months of virtual study. Despite everything, there was a ray of optimism that this partial reopening would signal the start of a return to pre-pandemic routines for students nationwide, given the strict safety protocols in place and the prospect of in-person interactions with instructors and classmates.

Elena was nervous, but she was determined to use her college experience to its fullest and not allow her fears to get in the way. Carefully choosing each item as though they were charms endowed with the ability to protect her from the unknowns that awaited, she packed her luggage. She put a little picture of Peter among her possessions as a reminder of the love that kept her afloat in the middle of the whirlwind of emotions coursing through her.

Elena felt a wave of excitement and a hint of nervousness in her veins as she got on the bus from Soweto to Pretoria. She could hear her thoughts rushing against a calm soundtrack provided by the bus's steady hum and regular pace. As she peered out the window, she saw the busy streets of Soweto give way to the more sedate Pretoria suburbs. After the epidemic caused the closing of her institution, she had yearned to return, and with every mile that went by, she felt herself getting closer to the well-known sights and sounds of that campus.

Reflection moments were sprinkled throughout the trip, though. Elena found herself thinking about all of the difficulties and unknowns that awaited her as the bus travelled its well-travelled path. Will things on campus continue to be affected by the pandemic, or will the switch back to in-person instruction go smoothly? How about her beloved Peter, who was now pursuing his studies in Durban? There was supposed to be excitement upon her return, but instead of that, the gap between them weighed hard on her heart.

Elena was starting to feel excited, but she was unable to control it despite her misgivings. She felt comfortable and a part of the group as she thought of being among her friends and classmates again. She let her mind wander to the exciting college life she would soon be a part of, with its heated debates, late-night study sessions, and moments of laughing with her fellow students, while the bus chugged along.

Elena's nervousness had given way to a renewed sense of resolve by the time the bus eventually arrived in Pretoria. She experienced a spike of energy as she got off the bus and entered the busy downtown streets. She was eager to take on the challenges and experiences that awaited her as she moved closer and closer to the well-known sights and sounds of her college campus.

But a feeling of worry settled over her as she travelled to her college campus. Formerly a place of comfort and familiarity, the campus suddenly felt strange and exotic. She could feel the warmth of Peter's embrace and the echoes of their laughing in every place she turned. These were the recollections she had of her time spent with Peter.

Elena tried everything to get lost in the rush and bustle of college life, but she was unable to get rid of the emptiness that was eating away at her heart. His presence was a continual reminder of the hole that now loomed huge in her life, and the absence of Peter weighed hard on her thoughts. Elena tried her best, but she could never seem to concentrate on her studies since her mind kept returning to him.

Elena felt herself becoming agitated more and more as the days extended into weeks. The familiar faces of her friends and classmates served as daily reminders of the life she had left behind in Soweto, and the regularity of college life felt oppressive. The more time went by, the more she missed Peter; the pain was relentless and would not go away.

Elena had never had such a sense of emancipation as she did now that she was living outside of her hometown. Being free to wander the streets of Pretoria at her own pace, she discovered that her parents lived miles away in Soweto. She felt a thrill of excitement at the prospect of having the freedom to come and go as she wanted, a taste of independence she had long craved.

Elena decided to pay Peter a visit in Durban, determined to close the distance between them. She was excited and full of anticipation at the idea of seeing him again; the notion of being reunited with him was a ray of hope amid the depths of despair. She was determined to get a flight, so she started searching, her fingers trembling as she browsed the alternatives.

At last, she discovered a flight that met her requirements, arriving at Peter's door directly from Johannesburg to Durban. She purchased her ticket with a strong sense of resolve, and the email confirmation served as a physical reminder of the upcoming voyage. A flutter of exhilaration filled Elena's chest as she got ready to start this new chapter in her life; the promise of what lay ahead on the other side made her pulse race.

Excitement and anxiety mixed when Elena confided in a few close college friends about her unexpected trip. She was nervous about travelling alone. She revealed that she was going to fly to Durban without telling her parents, first taking a bus from Pretoria to Johannesburg. She wanted her close companions to be aware of her location in case something unexpected happened. Elena felt secure and at ease, as she set off on her trip because they soothed her and told her that they would watch out for her safety.

Elena carefully considered all the scenarios that may occur while she was away and made plans for each one of them. In order to be sure that her parents wouldn't notice she even made the effort to talk to the housekeeper. The housekeeper promised to keep Elena's identity a secret when she told her that she would be spending a few days in the city at a friend's house. Elena was reminded to take care of herself while she was away by the housekeeper, who also showed concern for her wellbeing. Thankful for her compassion and support, Elena gave the housekeeper her word that she would.

Elena had been experiencing a swirl of mixed emotions in the days before her departure. A wave of anxiety pulled at her resolve, even as excitement coursed through her veins at the prospect of being with Peter again. She was nervous about their connection and the idea of working through its difficulties face-to-face, but her resolve did not waver. She set off on her adventure with careful preparation and the resolute support of her college mates, her heart full of hope and expectation. Elena's resolve grew stronger as the bus travelled along the familiar path, bringing her closer to her goal with every mile that went by. She was determined to face the obstacles that lay ahead. She was drawn nearer to the one she loved with each breath, the power of her everlasting affection and the prospect of a bright future providing her with hope and optimism.

Chapter - 21
A Day of Rediscovery

The flight to Durban left the soft embrace of early morning and descended over a canvas of predawn hues. A mixture of weariness and tangible excitement surrounded Elena's arrival, which was greeted by the gentle sighs of the airport as it awakened at four in the morning. She felt an ocean of emotions seething inside of her, and the quiet of the airport at such an early hour contrasted strongly.

It was a poetic turn of events that Elena chose to stay in a hotel that was conveniently near the airport and, ironically, just next door to Peter's house. Being so close added a complex level of symbolism and intimacy to their planned reunion and prepared the ground for a deep examination of their renewed bond. A special combination of emotional closeness and the essential space needed for healing and rediscovery was provided by the hotel's location, which was both close to and remote from Peter's daily life.

The minutes before their reunion seemed to go on forever, with anticipation building with every second that went by. It seemed as if the light had really broken when Peter eventually emerged through the arrival gates at six in the morning. Their kiss, soft and full of promise, said volumes about enduring love, forgiveness, and the unspoken promises of a future reinvented. Their hug was instantaneous and charged with the lightning of reconnection.

The small distance but significant importance of their journey from the airport to the hotel served as a quiet tribute to the range of emotions that were coursing through Elena's heart. A bittersweet mix of optimism and melancholy was evoked at the sight of Peter's house, so familiar but suddenly alienated by their chosen site of reunion. Peter expressed real joy upon receiving Elena's little but important present of chocolates from Johannesburg; it was a delightful prologue to the emotional feast that was to come.

Elena couldn't help but feel a surge of excitement as they walked inside the hotel room in the morning. With a massive king-sized bed in the middle and a gorgeous view of the city, the room was magnificent. Peter wrapped Elena into a close embrace as they enjoyed the scenery, and they planted their first kiss of the day.

As they intensified their kiss, their bodies pushed close to one another and their lips moved in perfect rhythm. Elena knew that this was going to be a memorable weekend since she could feel her pulse pounding. Elena could sense the fire between them as they broke the kiss, and Peter's eyes glowed with want.

They were enveloped by a bubble of solitude and exclusivity as they got comfortable in their room and the city began to gently come to life around them. Being able to negotiate the complicated details of their relationship without external constraints was made possible by this haven.

Each thing they said that morning was a deliberate step towards understanding and mending one another. Their chats were like a mosaic. Their hotel room became a hallowed place for vulnerability, hope, and shared dreams; it was an emotionally charged, neutral space set against the background of Peter's neighbouring home.

Peter drew Elena into an embrace that expressed all he felt as they stood on the balcony. It was Peter, who made the first move, taking Elena in his arms and carrying her to the bed with care. His hands caressed her body as he hovered over her, laying her down on the plush white sheets. Looking up at Peter, Elena's eyes glowed with need and her heart began to race with expectation.

Peter bent down to plant his lips on Elena's mouth once more, running his tongue over each hollow of her lips. As Elena felt Peter's body beneath his shirt, she let out a sigh of pleasure and ran her hands over his body. While their lips remained in contact, Elena felt the warmth spreading between her legs as Peter's hands began to slide down her body.

Peter moved away, surprising Elena by removing a pack of condoms from his backpack. Something was about to get very serious between the two of them, so she was excited and surprised at the same time as she stared at him. The passion between them was too great to ignore, even if they had not intended to go this far.

Taking Elena's jeans down her legs, Peter took the lead, his powerful hands working fast to undo the buttons. As soon as she emerged from them, her elegant black panties, which were already wet with expectation, showed. Sliding his hands up her legs and rubbing his fingers across the plush fabric, Peter's eyes grew black with need.

While Peter's t-shirt was being removed and thrown away, Elena's hands were also occupied. She felt the muscles of his toned chest strain beneath her hands, and she couldn't help but run them over it. Her fingers stumbling with the zip, she unzipped his jeans with great anticipation to take them off.

Their excitement was almost buzzing as they stood before each other in their underwear. After a while, Peter lost all self-control and drew Elena into an intense kiss, stroking and exploring every part of her body.

When Elena felt Peter's hands glide down to her pants and tease the material between her legs, she moaned into his mouth. His solid length was released as she went for his boxers' waistband and tugged them down. Their bodies ached to be together as they stood naked in front of one other, their breathing becoming laboured.

Peter ripped open the pack and slid the condom onto his solid shaft without a word. With great eagerness, Elena watched as he slipped between her legs and, in an instant, he was within her. As their bodies merged and they began to move in perfect time, they both let out a cry of pleasure.

With a moan of pleasure, Elena put her legs around Peter's waist and pulled him in. Elena could feel the tension rising inside her as their bodies moved in perfect rhythm. Her skin was massaged by Peter's hands as they moved over her body, making her feel intensely lustful.

Peter shifted positions as the tension increased, and Elena ended up on top, riding him wildly. Her body was burning with pleasure; she could feel every bit of him inside of her. They just kept moving in a pair, experimenting with various postures while they examined one another's bodies.

They continued to be engrossed in each other as the morning gave way to the afternoon, their bodies entwined and their desire intensifying with each passing second. After taking a short break, they returned to the room and couldn't take their hands off one other.

After sharing a passionate kiss, Elena and Peter curled up under the cosy blankets, feeling pleased and weary. As they hugged and revelled in the aftermath of their intense experience, their bodies became interconnected and their breathing rhythmic. They knew they were inseparable and that their love was strong as they looked into one other's eyes. Their thing was romance, and they both took great pleasure in their intense emotions for one another. The sound of their bellies grumbling served as a reminder that it was time for lunch as the two of them held each other longer, engrossed in the ecstasy of their love.

A straightforward but meaningful act of unity, lunch was served in the silence of their room. Although the lunch itself was unremarkable, it carried great meaning because of the tales and laughs that were exchanged, as well as the unsaid ties of rekindled friendship.

Then they were off to the shower, where they had a steaming, nude shower together, the warm water tumbling over their pressed bodies. Their hands wandered freely, exploring every inch of the body, they couldn't help but sneak kisses in between body washes.

When they had finished drying off from the shower, Peter ordered a cake. The most touching moment of their day came when he revealed his painstakingly prepared surprise—a cake in honour of Elena's upcoming birthday. Filled with forethought and excitement, the cake served as a vivid representation of their shared optimism and steadfast determination to create a future bright with challenges and joys that they would all experience together.

Melodic sounds of a gently sung birthday song accompanied their momentary transformation from their surroundings into an arena of pure joy and togetherness as they shared the cake. This small but meaningful gesture demonstrated the continuing strength of love, the value of special times spent together, and the possibility of fresh starts.

Once the cake had been gobbled up, they returned to the bed because they were unable to resist each other any longer. They explored one other's body and enjoyed every minute as they went slowly this time. They tried out crazy and adventurous stances they had never tried before, kissing, touching, and caressing one other in a flurry of desire.

Elena and Peter fell asleep naked, cuddled up in each other's arms, with a satisfaction that only comes from a day filled with passionate love-making. They had no plans for the evening, but they knew that they would spend it together, enjoying each other's company and exploring their love even more. As they drifted off to sleep, they knew that this was just the beginning of a beautiful journey together.

The day, a seamless blend of ordinary moments and extraordinary emotions, culminated in a series of heartfelt conversations and some wild events. These dialogues and moments, reflective and forward-looking, wove a tapestry of dreams, aspirations, and the shared reality of their journey ahead.

After all of the activities and talks, Peter and Elena had a romantic meal in the dimly lit room, where the atmosphere was just as warm as the dialogue that flowed between them. The table was tastefully laid, and every dish evoked a sense of intimacy and captured the delight of their shared experience. The sound of clinking glasses was accompanied by laughter, signifying moments they desired would stay forever. With a heart full of soft feelings, Peter said farewell to Elena as the night became darker and promised to return as soon as morning broke. As he drove home beneath the starry sky, he couldn't help but look forward to seeing Elena again in the early hours of the morning, the promise of their future encounter hanging in the air.

Elena's thoughts turned the day's events into a treasured story that woven itself into the details of their most recent romantic meal as she lay in bed. She fell asleep thinking about the ease with which they had reunited earlier, the challenges they had overcome together, and the road ahead. It was not just her birthday, but also a moving recognition of the revival of their love. It was characterised by newly made commitments and a deeper comprehension that had been confirmed in the soft light of the dinner's atmosphere. With her heart full and her mind at peace from the knowledge of the love and commitment that united them, Elena was ready to welcome whatever the morning light would bring as the silence of the night engulfed her.

On the second day of their reunion, Elena was sound asleep, worn out from the excitement and emotional turmoil of the day before, as the first rays of daylight peeked through the curtains. There was a persistent knock on the door, breaking the unexpected calm of the hotel room. Elena moved groggily towards the door, her eyes barely open, only to find herself engulfed in a firm hug as soon as it opened. Peter stood there, hugging her with an intensity that betrayed his intense adoration. With a riot of colours that appeared to illuminate the entire room, he carried a bouquet of roses in his hands.

Their days-long separation vanished with a single kiss as they sat on the bed's edge after exchanging gentle pleasantries for a little while. Peter was shocked to see that something was wrong as their reunion grew more intense. The way Elena's body felt against his was strangely warm. He withdrew to have a closer look at her, and concern rapidly appeared on his face. It was true; Elena had a fever that would not go away.

Peter acted without thinking for a second. He rushed out of the room, trying to find the closest pharmacy with his head racing. He quickly grabbed all the medications Elena would require for a full recovery. He went back into the room and assumed the job of caretaker, which he did with love and sincerity.

While this was going on, Elena was struck both immensely affected by Peter's quick and unshakable support and overwhelmed by the unexpected turn of events. With gentle care and tenderness, her head was propped up on Peter's lap. Peter fed her chocolates in between prescription dosages, hoping that the small treat would cheer her up from her feverish condition.

He spent hours sitting with her, his presence a reassuring constant while he ordered food that would be easy on her system and comforted her with cold cloths to lower her temperature.

Peter was quite careful while choosing the proper meal for Elena since he saw how important it was to feed her, particularly given her current condition of weakness. In an attempt to stimulate her hunger and provide some solace amongst the agony of her sickness, he placed an order for her favourite meal for lunch. Elena took comfort from the comforting flavours, even though she was feverish; every mouthful brought back memories of Peter's kindness and their happy times together.

With the afternoon drawing near, the knowledge that Elena would soon be leaving them loomed large over their makeshift haven. Elena had a hassle-free ride to the airport thanks to Peter's advance reservation of a taxi, the ever-watchful spouse. Her health was partially restored, and her baggage packed, they walked to the taxi, hands bound together both of them dreading their upcoming farewell.

Peter continued to show concern and care even at the airport. He stayed by Elena's side, helping her check-in and making sure she had all she needed for a relaxing journey. There were whispered prayers and quiet vows to be back together soon throughout the wait, which made it bittersweet.

Elena turned to face Peter as she eventually arrived at the departure gate, and he was observing her with a mixture of pride and worry in his gaze. That day and time had shown their bond—one bolstered by compassion, empathy, and unwavering support—to be stronger than ever. Given how unique and priceless what they had was, Elena's heart was full of love and thankfulness.

Beyond simply being a loving partner, Peter's deeds included deep engagement, as seen by the colourful flowers and his careful attention to detail. Elena felt a strong sense of comfort and admiration for the guy who had supported her during a time of vulnerability since their dedication to one another had been renewed in good times and bad.

Elena was thinking of Peter as the plane lifted off, cherished by the recollections of the previous two days. Even though the illness was unpleasant, it showed how deeply they were connected, so their goodbye was not a final one but a sign of more to come. She phoned Peter as soon as the plane touched down in Johannesburg, and his eagerness to speak with her conveyed his genuine concern for her well. Though she felt at ease in his care, the drive to Pretoria from Johannesburg was tinged with fatigue, leaving Elena longing for some peaceful time alone while Peter kept checking in.

She was grateful for Peter's attention to detail, but she was also a little irritated. She longed for sleep, a moment's respite from the chaotic swirl of feelings and exhaustion. Nevertheless, every call she received from Peter showed his care, which radiated warmth and served as a constant reminder of his love, despite their physical separation.

Elena said softly, trying to strike a balance between her desire for rest and appreciating his worry, "I appreciate your concern, Peter. But, I'll call you when I arrive in Pretoria." Her gentle comments signalled the end of their talk and gave her permission to sink into the solitude of her journey.

Elena thought about how close their relationship was, how it had been forged by hardships and brightened by tender and understanding times, as theb us buzzed its way towards Pretoria. After a short while, the annoyance vanished and was replaced with a deep gratitude for having Peter in her life. In spite of the uncertainty of distance and the hope of future reunions, his love, a steadfast light, gave her comfort.

When she finally arrived in Pretoria, the city's familiarity welcomed her and excited her for the life that lay ahead. The fact that Peter's love persisted as a constant companion is evidence of their strong relationship. Their story—one of love overcoming the challenges of distance and personal development—kept on developing as a result of their courage and continuous support.

With the hardships and care of the day strengthening her love for Peter, she looked forward to the day they would be reunited, stronger and more in love than ever. Her love for Peter rose as high as the jet that flew her away. This thorough story paints a realistic image of a partnership that adversity only helps to deepen, capturing not just the events of a single day but also the spirit of a love-filled, caring, and unshakeable support-filled connection.

Chapter - 22
Veils of Silence and Shadows of Doubt

Elena's period of normalcy was short-lived as the upsurge in her emotions was reflected in the outside world, following her brief return to Pretoria. She found herself stuck on familiar ground but feeling lost as word broke of the college closures, a ripple effect of the continuous struggle against an invisible foe. Now, the digital classroom loomed over her again, a reminder of the distance that kept her apart from Peter. The temporary reprieve in the shape of restored educational institutions had been a failed experiment in the face of a relentless pandemic.

She had grown all too familiar with the dance with shadows, and her return to Soweto was shrouded in mystery. Her recent adventure to Durban had been surrounded by a web of falsehoods that she had so carefully crafted, so the idea of being discovered at the airport had been a persistent worry in the back of her mind. The traces of passion Peter had left on her skin served as a physical memory of their times together, but fortunately, luck—or perhaps fate—had been on her side and she returned home unharmed.

Elena's father, Miguel, was not a talker and showed even less sign of amazement. But nothing escaped his watchful eyes—not the tired relief in Elena's stance upon her return, nor the telltale marks of a youthful love engraved on her neck. He made the decision to keep quiet, acting as a silent protector of his daughter's secrets and maybe knowing more than he said. This unwritten contract between the father and the daughter was a sign of their link and a strand of trust in their relationship.

Her mother, Carla, saw the hickeys right away because she had the sharp eye of someone who had experienced the rough seas of love. Miguel responded to her questioning with promptness, which seemed to be a sign of worry. The straightforward advice he gave Elena—to take care of her hunger—acted as a barrier against the torrent of inquiries Carla had prepared for. Elena realised then that her parents had made a secret agreement that served as a barrier between them and the harsh realities of life.

Elena was soothed by Peter's words that evening as the shadows moved over the walls of her childhood room, providing comfort from the pain of being apart. She talked about the things that had happened that day, the wall of silence her father had put around her secret, and the reluctant protective cloak her mother had put on. They were separated by a physical boundary, but their laughing filled the digital space between them.

The days that ensued served as evidence of how flexible youthful love can be. They frequently engaged in co-viewing, exchanging laughter and tears over films viewed together over screen share, making the distance between them feel a bit less scary. They also played online games together with digital avatars, and made late-night calls. Still, behind the surface of this new normal, the shadows of insecurity were feeding the seeds of mistrust sown by previous betrayals, which started to blossom again.

The trust was ripped apart once more during one of their movie evenings, a ritual that had grown to be essential to their relationship. Elena hardly used a social networking app, but one harmless pop-up while watching movies with Peter as he was sharing his screen notice turned out to be the starting point for Peter's broken promises. The communication, evidently from his previous partner, struck like a sledgehammer to the delicate trust they had been reestablishing. Peter's hurried attempts to change the subject and cover up the proof of his continuous contact with his past with a mountain of justifications did nothing but widen the hole in his doubts.

Elena's fears collided with Peter's barriers in a storm of a confrontation that took place. Elena felt like she was being squeezed by a chilly hand as he reluctantly consented to have contact under the pretext of friendship. The outcry of betrayal in her veins overpowered the explanations and reasons, and they were all met with silence.

This information served as a mirror for Elena, reflecting her deepest worries and feelings of uncertainty towards the girl who had previously been Peter's sweetheart. Her pain stemmed not from the communication, but rather from the concealment and realisation that Peter had once again chosen to balance between the truth and falsehoods, erring on the side of deception.

Following their fight, there was a gulf filled with the reverberations of their dispute that became colder in the digital realm between them. Elena was forced to choose between the hurt of Peter's treachery and the love she still had for him. She carried a great deal of weight over the uncertainty of their future—a route veiled in silence and shadows.

Elena struggled to make a decision as the days stretched into weeks. Already crooked and weathered, the foundations of their relationship looked ready to give way. However, optimism lingered within her, unyielding like a lighthouse in the night.

Her talks with Peter started to resemble a dance around the big issue in the room, with their words carefully navigating the minefield that stood in their way. The easygoing conversation and laughing that had previously defined their exchanges had become strained, a mask worn over the cracks in their bond that had grown. Nonetheless, a resolute spark of hope refused to go out in Elena's heart despite the uncertainties and betrayal's sorrow.

The gap and stillness between them widened as the days blended into weeks. Elena immersed herself in her studies, taking comfort in the structure and diversions provided by online learning. However, during their alone time, her mind would always return to Peter, their shared experiences, and the searing sense of betrayal that had scarred her heart forever.

Elena's phone rang one evening while she was sitting there staring out her window at the setting sun casting the sky a pink and orange haze. Peter was the one. When she answered the phone, her stomach knotted with a mixture of fear and eagerness, making her heart skip a beat.

The voice of Peter, who had formerly been a comfort, appeared to reverberate far away. He talked about his guilt, about how painful it was to be apart from her, and about his undying love for her. He begged for pardon, for the opportunity to make a fresh start, to put what was destroyed back together. Elena took in the words as they poured out of his heart, a tapestry of regret and desire that Elena silently observed.

At the conclusion of the call, pledges of openness and confidence were made, marking a first step in the direction of reconciliation. However, as Elena lay in bed that night, the weight of their talk bearing down on her, she came to the realisation that trust could not simply be restored, nor could forgiveness be turned on and off. Once developed, the wounds of betrayal persisted and cast dark shadows over the prospect of fresh starts.

Elena and Peter set out on a precarious path of recovery in the weeks that followed. Talks that had previously been tense and full of unresolved issues gradually started to soften and reveal vulnerable and understanding moments. They discussed their aspirations, their concerns, and the lessons they had discovered throughout the trial by fire of their breakup.

However, notwithstanding their slow progress towards one another, the ghost of the past remained there, serving as a continual reminder of how easily trust may be betrayed. The want to move on from the memories of deceit was matched with the opposing forces of love and hurt that Elena found herself struggling with.

Signs of healing were also seen in the outer world during this phase of hesitant reconciliation. As instances decreased and life slowly started to resume its regular rhythms, the pandemic's unrelenting march paused and gave way to cautious hope.

Elena was excited and nervous at the same time when her institution announced that in-person classes may resume. It was a sign of normalcy. The idea of going back to university and experiencing the life of a college student again seemed like a welcome relief from the exhaustion of living alone. Nonetheless, it also meant facing the truth about her connection with Peter in a society where social distance and lockdowns were no longer constraints.

Elena was at a crossroads as the day she was supposed to return to college became closer. She had been put to the test during the last several months as she travelled through the darkness of uncertainty and the anguish of betrayal, discovering the extent of her love and forgiveness for Peter. Her heart bore a map of the challenging terrain they had traversed together, marked with the wounds from that adventure.

However, Elena realised that although while the voyage with Peter had been difficult at times, it had also been a time of significant personal growth as she prepared to pack her things and return to the outside world. She had found a strength she didn't know she had in the furnace of their tribulations, a strength forged in the fire of grief and recovery.

There remained uncertainty in the path ahead, with the past's shadows never far behind. However, Elena came forth with a calm resolution, a will to meet the future with open arms, and the belief that her and Peter's love, tempered by the hardships of their separation, would prove resilient enough to withstand any adversity.

Elena looked out the window as the scenery passed by in a swirl of browns and greens as she boarded the bus to return to Pretoria. She pondered on Peter, the assurances they had exchanged, and the shared future they intended to create. A tiny glimmer of hope flared in her heart, illuminating the way ahead and serving as a beacon to help her find her way home.

Chapter - 23
Bridges and Brews: Exploring Bonds and Boundaries

The gentle rays of the late afternoon light bathed Elena's room as she skillfully folded her garments and packed them into her luggage. Every article of clothing seemed like a missing component from her life, which was now dispersed around Pretoria and Soweto. She thought of Mike and Rachel, her new pals from the virtual world of late-night study sessions and college projects, as she zipped the suitcase shut. Their friendship, which was forged virtually but unproven in the real world, was a bright spot amidst the ominous pandemic clouds.

Then her phone rang and the screen lit up with a message from Rachel saying, "Can't wait to finally meet you! I'm hosting dinner tonight." Elena's tummy danced with a mixture of nervousness and exhilaration. She hoped for and feared the day she would finally meet Rachel in person since it would mean bridging the virtual and the real.

Elena found herself sitting opposite Rachel in a cosy corner of a busy restaurant as the twilight shadows became longer. The warmth of their memories of their online adventures and their shared laughing soon dispelled the uneasiness that had first arisen. Their phones were abandoned next to their plates, a reminder of the bond that remained even in the face of digital distance. Elena felt like she belonged again as they said their goodbyes and had their night captured on camera for all time. However, behind her happiness, there was a stream of unhappiness rising.

Her uneasiness suddenly surged upon hearing Peter's voice, which had before been a ray of hope. She felt deep doubts pierced in her heart by his careless remarks about his former girlfriend, the evenings spent in clouds of smoke and the sound of glasses clinking. Elena took great delight in her comprehension and her readiness to acknowledge Peter's shortcomings. Her quiet, however, was weighed down by a thick veil of unease and worry as the days prolonged into weeks.

Their disagreements had turned into a recurrent theme, getting more and more discordant as they went along. The most recent had erupted over a mere announcement of Elena's intention to meet Mike. "Why do you need to meet him? Isn't talking to me enough?" Peter said, his words cutting and accusatory as they echoed in her ears. Elena couldn't help but feel furious about his position due to its duplicity considering his personal relationships and connections. Nevertheless, she hung up, their furious conversation coming to an abrupt stop with the dial tone.

Elena was feeling stormy, but Mike's motorbike arrived with a calm hum. At the sight of her troubled forehead, his easy grin faded. "Everything okay?" he said, his worry genuine.

Elena said softly, "I just need to get away for a bit," amidst the chaos of her thoughts.

Elena flatly denied any alcohol consumption when Mike asked about it. She claimed that she doesn't drink. Persistently pushing her to give it a try, Mike continued, maybe detecting some underlying tension in her. At first, Elena was reluctant to give in and stuck to her convictions. But over time, her resistance was worn down by the weight of her disappointments and the attraction of a little reprieve from her troubles. Elena gave in to Mike's prodding with a sigh of resignation, seeing that she might use alcohol—an old treatment for stress relief—to ease her burden.

The pub they picked was a dark haven from the outer world. Elena resisted Mike's offer to have a drink, a struggle she ultimately lost to the prospect of momentary freedom. Elena found herself opening up to Mike and sharing her feelings as the amber liquid flowed through her, untying the knots in her stomach. A flood of anxieties, annoyances, and the searing openness of her love for Peter spilled out in her remarks. In the midst of her emotional turmoil, Mike listened and acted as a quiet rock, comprehending instead of passing judgment.

Their discourse wandered over the intricacies of interpersonal relationships, touching on topics such as trust, personal development, and the bravery required to be genuinely honest with oneself and others. Elena had a weird clarity despite the turmoil of her emotions as the night became darker and the last of the beer was consumed. Even if Mike's viewpoint differed from her own, it illuminated previously unexplored avenues for her to manage her connection with Peter without compromising her mental well-being.

The noise of the bar contrasted sharply with the quiet that greeted her upon returning home. Peter's physical and emotional absence left a glaring hole and served as a sharp reminder of their growing separation. For the first time, Elena wasn't sure whether she wanted him to call or message, and he hadn't.

The following several days passed quickly as she focused on herself and her routine, with the online lessons acting as a pleasant diversion from her turbulent thoughts. But the unspoken conflict with Peter continued to haunt her like a shadow, something she could never fully accept or reject.

In the middle of her mental anguish, she had decided to meet Mike in order to find some sort of diversion and some sense of normalcy. However, it had now turned into a crucial instance, a defining event that made her face the truth about her relationship with Peter. It was difficult for her to accept that she had started to restrict herself, to shape her words and deeds to fit inside Peter's predetermined parameters.

The argument with Peter was a sign of larger problems, of basic disagreements between their conceptions of freedom and trust, and it was based on his hypocrisy and her desire for real connection. Elena has always taken great satisfaction in her openness and her conviction that an honest relationship is essential to a happy one. But there was a gap that appeared to be growing bigger every day between them—Peter was unable to give her the same freedom and trust.

After a while, the days turned into weeks, and Elena was left standing. There was no denying her love for Peter; it was a profound, enduring bond that had withstood many adversities. However, she came to the realisation that love was not a cure-all for all relationship problems. When trust was damaged, it was difficult to rebuild, and the lingering effects of previous betrayals created difficult-to-disprove concerns.

She did not make the decision to face Peter and reveal her vulnerabilities and concerns lightly. It was a leap of faith, an expectation that their love would be able to cut through hurt and misunderstanding. A delicate ballet of words and a negotiation of emotions to find common ground amid the wreckage of past conflicts characterised the talk that followed.

Elena's personal distress was reflected in Peter's reaction, which was a mixture of defensiveness and sincere regret. The wounds that had festered in silence were soothed by his admittance of his mistakes and his promise to work towards improving his comprehension of and respect for her sentiments.

Still, there was a lingering feeling of worry as Elena hung up the phone. No matter how earnest, promises lacked substance unless they were accompanied by deeds. Rebuilding trust was a difficult and drawn-out process that required tolerance, empathy, and most of all, a willingness to change.

In the weeks that followed, Elena and Peter cautiously and optimistically sailed across the perilous seas of their love. There were lapses in judgment and resentments that came to the surface, but there were also times of deep connection and visions of a day when love and trust would live in peace.

Elena also developed friendships with Mike and Rachel, which proved that close friendships might enhance rather than worsen an individual's relationship with Peter. She laughed and felt comforted in their presence, and it served as a reminder of the many ways love had shown itself in her life.

The future was full of unknowns, like a wide ocean in front of Elena as she stood on the brink of a new chapter. However, equipped with the knowledge gained from the past, the backing of her friends, and a shaky ceasefire with Peter, she moved on with optimism in her heart.

The path ahead was unclear, and given their common past, the result of her and Peter's efforts was in doubt. Elena discovered a strength she was unaware she had, though, in the act of trying, in the everyday decision to love, forgive, and develop.

She was confident that she would confront whatever was ahead of her with fortitude, led by the light of her own inner truth. She had learned the importance of self-respect and the bravery needed to ask for the love and trust she deserved from the experience. Elena realised as she turned to face the horizon that she would follow the route with integrity, head held high and spirit intact, no matter where it lead.

Chapter - 24
Peter's Aloofness and Mike's Friendship

Elena found herself navigating a narrative she hadn't imagined as the days unfolded like the pages of an unread book. Peter, who had once been her ray of hope among the storm of her life, had become a vessel that passed by at night, his presence more ethereal than real. Elena was left to float in the emptiness of his disregard while his world revolved around a constellation of female friends and his enduring ties to his ex. With her heart bleeding for the Peter she knew in the past, she attempted to cling to the semblance of their relationship.

Elena submitted to Peter's changing attitudes not out of ignorance but rather because of a deep-seated worry that a confrontation would break their eroding relationship. Every time Peter told stories of his adventures, she felt a silent storm building inside of her, a tempest of loneliness and anxiety she dared not speak. Though it left her alone in her own relationship, her silence was a sacrifice and a sign of her unwavering devotion.

Elena discovered Mike to be an unexpected confidante during this emotional upheaval. After their conversation veered off into the subject of rebellion one evening, Elena made an impetuous suggestion. With a hint of curiosity and urgency in her voice, she asked, "Have you ever smoked?" Mike and she were both astonished by a proposal that followed her own declaration of innocence. With a mix of indignation and vulnerability in her voice, she said, "Let's try it together." The suggestion was not merely to smoke; it was a cry for help, a brief respite from the bonds of her mental prison.

They were as foolish as they were sincere in their attempt to enter the world of smoking. With all of its options, the smoke shop was like entering a forbidden place. The act itself was an awkward dance of laughs and coughs, a shared experience that briefly lifted Elena's heart's shadows. However, the light was fleeting, as the burden of her guilt cast a shadow over it.

With the expectation that being honest would help them overcome their differences, the confession to Peter was an outpouring of reality. She had long ignored the double standards, though, and Peter's response served as a mirror for them. An unexpected realisation of their relationship's imbalance was his outrage over her single infraction in the context of his own freedoms. She realised that her sacrifices had been one-sided, and their quarrel exposed the cracks in their relationship and the injustice of his demands.

Driven by love and hope, Elena set out on her trips to Durban in an effort to heal the wounds that had been inflicted upon her and to locate the Peter she had fallen in love with amidst the rubble of his scorn. Peter's excuses, disguised as limitations imposed by his parents, paled in comparison to her dedication, which was demonstrated on every trip. In stark contrast to Peter's indifference, Mike's care and his words ensuring her safety stood out. Accepting that her value was determined by her ability to satisfy his needs, rather than by her own, was a painful pill to swallow.

Elena struggled with the conflicting sentiments she had for Peter as she lay awake in the early morning hours, the stillness of her chamber broken only by the cadence of her thoughts. She came to see that love was more than just the existence of affection; it also involved the reciprocation of respect and care, qualities that had started to decline in the wake of Peter's behaviour. She came to the harsh and uncompromising realisation that her road of dedication had been a solitary one, her efforts unrewarded, her love unreturned in proportion to its giving.

Mike's concern stood in stark contrast to Peter's lack of it, and his support during these turbulent times turned into a ray of friendship. Elena started to doubt the fundamental foundation of her relationship with Peter during these instances of sincere concern from Mike. Was their love strong enough to make up for their differences in dedication? Was the reality of her loss of identity hidden by her fear of losing Peter?

Their disagreements with Peter, which used to be infrequent thunderstorms, had now taken on a life of their own, with every quarrel destroying the foundation of their love. Elena's act of defiance against the limitations of her situation, her choice to smoke with Mike, had been a request for understanding and a test of Peter's empathy. However, his response did little more than emphasise the distance that was opening up between them—a gap that was stoked by Peter's demands of Elena's behaviour that were not met by her own.

In the economy of Peter's affections, Elena's sacrifices, her visits to Durban, her financial and emotional investments, were all considered as tokens of love that were never appreciated. It was an unpleasant shock to see how unappreciated and undetected her efforts were. Elena had travelled far for love, but Peter, rooted by lame justifications and a lack of initiative, had not moved an inch.

Elena found support from Mike, but it wasn't a substitute for what she wanted from Peter; rather, it was a mirror reflecting what she was entitled to consideration, consideration, and recognition. The inadequacies in Peter's treatment of her were highlighted by Mike's straightforward questions concerning her safety and his readiness to listen without passing judgment.

As Elena struggled to process these facts and felt the weight of unfulfilled hopes and unacknowledged love, she came to the realisation that she had to face the truth about her connection with Peter. The loss of happiness and self-worth seemed a worse evil than the dread of losing him, which had previously controlled her behaviour.

In the quiet of reflection, Elena had the courage to tell Peter what she needed and expected from him—she wanted the same thoughtfulness and deference that she had always shown him. Even though it was likely to be painful, this conversation was also a step towards her agency being reclaimed, a statement that she was no longer going to be a victim in a relationship that made her less of a light.

Their relationship's future was in doubt, and the outcome of this confrontation was unclear. Elena, however, was unwavering in her resolve to advocate for herself and look for a love that was not just declared but really lived. Elena had a flash of insight when she realised that a love that respected limits, returned sacrifices, and recognised her value was a relationship worth having.

Even though the road ahead was full of unknowns, Elena was resolved to face it with dignity, whether it meant moving on from her relationship with Peter or setting out on a new adventure by herself. She had learned from her experiences how important it is to respect oneself and others in any relationship.

Elena felt calm among the chaos as the sun rose on a new day, spilling golden hues across her room. She'd spoken out about her needs, faced her concerns, and—most importantly—started the healing process. Elena was confident that she would come out stronger, her heart unbroken, and her spirit unbroken, no matter where the road with Peter took her. Whether it went on or not, her voyage with Peter had been a chapter in her story, but it would not become the story. Elena was prepared to move on and embrace the future with a heart wide open to love, but she also had the discernment to look for a partner who would elevate, value, and respect her true self.

Elena's love for Peter was a monument to her inner strength; it was so strong and unshakable that it overcame mistreatment and misunderstanding. Though Peter often seemed to blame her for the shortcomings in their relationship, Elena was the one who strengthened their bond time and time again with her forgiveness and patience. She made the decision to ignore Peter's actions, which caused her great pain and planted uncertainty and loneliness in the garden of her heart. But she loved him anyway, with a tenacity that was both her strength and her weakness. Even though Peter didn't realise the damage his own actions had created, her efforts were the glue holding the pieces of their dying love together.

During her calm moment of reflection, Elena realised that her love, albeit unconditional and wide, had turned into a mute observer of her own happiness's decline. She came to see that in her efforts to make their relationship stronger, she had neglected the fundamentals of respect and understanding between them. A turning point was her sad admission that she had been struggling alone to save what was left of their love. It made sense of the disarray of her feelings and showed her the way to respect and self-love. Elena's experience with love had taught her that the real power of a relationship is not how long a person can suffer in silence but rather how courageous they are to look for happiness and contentment in themselves as well as in others.

Chapter - 25
Elena's Journey Through Hope and Heartbreak

Elena, fuelled by hope and a longing for closure, decided to go to Durban, seeking to uncover if the embers of love with Peter still burned. As the plane dropped into Durban, Elena's heart was full of eager anticipation. Although she had not decided to give her relationship with Peter another go lightly, the idea of spending time with him, getting to know him and his loved ones, and experiencing his world all felt like a ray of optimism in the middle of the uncertainty that had surrounded their relationship. The Durban sun felt as warm as she felt when she got off the plane, a silent promise of fresh starts.

She had not expected such a warm welcome from Peter. Elena had long desired to be a part of the picture of household bliss that his family's introduction to her and their shared dinners where laughter flowed abundantly like wine portrayed. Her weary heart found solace in Peter's attentions, the candies that demonstrated his comprehension of her preferences, and the flowers that appeared to encapsulate his love itself. Elena allowed herself to hope for a future in which the love she freely offered would be returned with an equally passionate outpouring during those brief days.

She felt welcomed into not only their home but also their lives by his mother's kindness towards her. Elena became more and more woven into Peter's world—a world she had long desired to be a part of—with every smile and every tale they exchanged. Her heart was full, assured that Peter loved her just as much and without reservation as she did, as she boarded the plane headed back to Soweto.

The return to Soweto was a return to reality, but it was a reality Elena felt ready to face, fortified by the memories of her visit. But the sharp contrast between the love Peter had shown and what he said next would crush her newly acquired self-assurance. Elena thought she might never fully recover from the request for a breakup, given that it occurred so soon after their blissful days spent together.

As Elena struggled to make sense of the differences between Peter—who had shown her his family and had gazed at her with love—and Peter, who now spoke of ending their journey together, confusion was the order of the day. It felt unfair and cruel to him that he accused her of being dominating and putting limitations on him. For the sake of their love, hadn't she been the one to compromise and forgive his transgressions?

There was quiet in response to Elena's cries for an explanation, for anything that may explain the gap that had appeared between them out of the blue. There was an emptiness in the hollow chambers of her heart as she realised that Peter had stopped her, closing off any means of contact. At her most vulnerable, lying on the ground among the broken pieces of her dreams, Elena couldn't help but wonder if the sudden breakup was due to Peter's ex, the darkness that had hovered over their relationship the entire time.

In the last act that broke their last remaining ties, Peter blocked Elena from all of their active digital paths except the ones that remained untouched by their conversations, leaving her alone in a quiet that rang with the broken pieces of their broken love. The blocking seemed like the last act of betrayal, the last break in the bonds that had united them. Despite being aware of how his ex-girlfriend's actions fueled Elena's fears, Peter had never blocked her. It hurt more than words could express to be cast aside so quickly and totally. With no answers to the issues that plagued her and a future that appeared so bright now cast in shadows of loss and doubt, Elena was left to navigate the turbulent waters of her heartache on her own.

The anguish Elena felt changed into introspection as the days stretched into weeks. After being put to the test, her once-unwavering devotion for Peter had shown to be unsatisfactory. It was painful to acknowledge that her expectations had been based on the shaky foundation of Peter's love and that her dedication had been met with deceit. Still, Elena started to discover the germ of a fresh insight beneath this furnace of suffering.

It was a difficult road to return to oneself. Regaining her self-worth and moving past her relationship with Peter was a gradual process that involved every step she took away from the devastation of their relationship. The healing process was a gradual one, interspersed with periods of strength and clarity and moments of relapse into sadness.

Elena found stores of resilience in herself that she was unaware she had in the quiet of her recuperation. She started to realise that true love deserves respect in addition to the delight that it offers. It became a guiding light when she realised she deserved someone who would support her and wouldn't turn her fears against her.

Elena's story of finding serenity amid the turmoil of unrequited love and betrayal, and her journey from pain to healing, was a monument to her resilience. Her story would always include the wounds from her encounter with Peter, but they would never define her. Rather, they would serve as a constant reminder of her ability to hurt, love, and most importantly, to heal.

Despite being tested, Elena's soul remained unbroken and her heart remained receptive to the idea of love that would recognise and value her. She emerged from the storm with her worth unimpaired. Elena took a bold step forward, ready to face whatever lay ahead, even though the future was unknown and the route was unworn. In the end, her love story with Peter was but a chapter in the larger narrative of her life, a narrative that she now held the pen to write.

With her broken heart cast a shadow over everything, Elena's surroundings had become dull and lifeless. She was left floating in a sea of unanswered questions by Peter's abrupt choice to break up with her, a link she had created and believed in. The swirl of thoughts that plagued her did not stop, nor did his evasive and unconvincing reasons alleviate the pain in her heart. Having no idea why Peter had withdrawn, Elena was left in a state of indecision of her own choosing, unable to take any more action.

After a month in this sort of suspended animation, Elena decided she wanted to get closure the way she wanted it. She was desperate for clarification, desiring information as much as air, in the hopes that realising Peter's motivations would at last let her let go of her uncertainty and suffering. Her attempts to communicate with Peter were greeted with a wall of silence that she was unable to break through until she became desperate enough to look for other ways to express herself. Her last hope came from the email she sent, a digital message in a bottle thrown into the huge ocean of the internet. Peter's lukewarm response, an ambiguous agreement to possibly meet, was enough to set her course. She packed her bags and headed to Durban, holding onto the notion that meeting Peter in person would provide her the much-needed closure.

Lifted by a shaky hope, Elena came into the city, drawn in by Peter's hazy notion of a potential meeting. Unfortunately, the harsh truth hit her as soon as she arrived, and Peter's reply to her arrival was a stern "Who told you to come?" Her hope was dashed by his comments, which were spoken with a harsh dismissiveness that was like a blast of cold air. It seemed strange and alien to be in Durban, a city that had once stood for the reunion of hearts. Her unwinding took place in the white-painted, impersonal hotel room. A worse betrayal than the actual split was Peter's refusal to meet with her and his silence in the face of her vulnerability. Elena was alone in a city where the ghosts of her nightmares still resonated, and she felt the weight of her loneliness like never before. She was left breathing heavily due to the overwhelming reality of her circumstances as the tears began to fall, an outpouring of anguish and annoyance.

The worst ideas crept into her consciousness that evening, offering a long-term fix for her momentary suffering. However, there was a glimmer of hope even in the darkest recesses of her misery. She remembered Elodie and Mike, the cautions they had issued and their genuine concern for her. They would still be there when the storm had passed even though they had anticipated the storm's arrival much earlier than she had. She was pulled back from the brink by this realisation, the knowledge that she was not as alone as she felt.

Elena decided to leave Durban that very evening instead of continuing on with her scheduled two-day return trip. She was getting closer to the prospect of healing with each mile as she made her way back to her city, which was a haze of broken dreams. And in the silence of that return trip, I made up my mind to move on, really move on. Her search for Peter had only resulted in nothingness, but in the process she had come to terms with the fact that some questions can never be fully answered—not because of any malice, but rather because there are moments when there are no adequate excuses to heal a shattered heart.

The days and weeks that followed served as a tribute to Elena's inner strength, which had been overshadowed but never diminished by her love for Peter. She turned to Mike and Elodie, her friends, whose sympathy and encouragement gave her the starting point to reassemble her sense of self. Their friendship served as a constant in her life, untarnished by the complications of romantic love and a constant reminder that love could take many different forms and that each was valuable in and of itself.

It was a terrifying trip through the dark as Elena made her way through the hurt of her breakup and the shadow of her hopelessness in Durban. It was a tunnel, though, that led to light. After all, she came out on the other side with a stronger sense of her own value, a greater appreciation for herself, and the knowledge that sometimes finding closure requires giving yourself a gift.

She rediscovers loves and interests she had set aside in the chase of an unfulfilled love, finding comfort in things that had once made her happy. She painted, wrote poetry, and kept a journal, with every brushstroke and word serving as evidence of her recovery. She re-established her relationship with her family, finding solace in their unwavering love and support, and she created plans for the future that were unique to her and unrelated to anyone else.

Elena's narrative exemplifies perseverance and serves as a reminder that despite its fragility, the human heart is capable of extraordinary power. It is a tale of lost love as well as self-discovery and the arduous but necessary path from grief to recovery. Elena discovered that moving on meant more than simply letting go of the past; it also meant welcoming the future and being receptive to fresh opportunities, aspirations, and expressions of love.

Elena has a whole heart as she looks forward to the future—not because it was never broken, but rather because she had the guts to put it back together. Though it is not her whole narrative, her relationship with Peter will always be a part of her and a chapter in her life's book. Elena is still writing her story, and she is poised to write stories of adventure, love in all its manifestations, and hope in the pages.

Chapter - 26
Finding Peace and Purpose with Friends

Elena discovered that she was drawn to the energy of the evening and the company of her friends when her problematic relationship with Peter ended. She didn't realise how quickly things changed; every date, cigarette, and drink was a step towards a direction she had never imagined taking. It turned into a melancholy symphony of emancipation and escape, though, as she continued to live her new way of life.

Her constant companion in these nighttime adventures was Mike, the ever-loyal pal. They moved through the smoke-filled maze of clubs, the boisterous atmosphere of parties late into the night, and the quiet moments that said a thousand words together. The habit of smoking, which began as a once-in-a-lifetime pleasure, soon developed into a shared vice. Boxes of cigarettes would disappear as the subjects of conversation veered from the serious to the banal, with each puff providing a momentary solace from Elena's heartbreak.

However, there were drawbacks to this newly discovered independence. Elena and Mike stood out from the rest of their group because of their habits, which set them apart from Rachel, Elodie, and others who preferred moderation. Even though it was slight, this distinction gave their relationships more depth and became a thread that ran through their group dynamics. Rachel and Elodie were clean-living, but they never judged them; their acceptance was a testament to the strength of their bond.

Elena's days were a flurry of activity, a purposeful haze created to ward off the loneliness ghost. She found true moments of joy with Mike, Rachel, and Elodie; every outing was a mosaic of laughing and secrets exchanged. But as the light went down and the laughter subsided, the silence in her room served as a sharp reminder of the void that neither smoking nor partying could ever fully satisfy.

Though rare, disagreements with Mike started to intersperse their friendship. These arguments, which were frequently over insignificant issues, were like miniature storm clouds that would soon pass. Elodie would frequently make fun of their arguments with her lighthearted jokes;

her humour served as a comforting salve to patch things up and bring about harmony. Even though their arguments temporarily distanced them, they were never sufficient to sever their enduring friendship.

Elena's peer circle had a special dynamic that combined complexity and togetherness. Every person, with all of their peculiarities and attributes, added to a fabric full of variety and comprehension. The time we spent together was a treasured getaway, with hours passing into one another without the effects of time.

For Elena, though, the nights told a different tale. The quiet was heightened by her room's isolation, which stood in sharp contrast to the bustle of her days. During these peaceful times, her mind would become introspective, replacing the happiness of company with a reflection on her decisions. She hardly recognised the person she had become since drinking and smoking, which had once been her means of escape, now seemed like chains.

Her emotional landscape was wide, and the short-lived highs and dopamine spikes were like stars in the sky. She could still see the darkness at the edges, even with their light illuminating her route. While having friends like Mike, Rachel, and Elodie around offered comfort, Elena came to realise that the path to recovery was one she had to travel on her own.

Elena had to come to terms with this insight before she could appreciate the benefits of isolation as a place for reflection and personal development rather than as a gap to be filled with diversions. She learned perseverance, self-discovery, and the value of true connections from her arguments with Mike, her introspective nights, and her humorous days. All of these experiences were interwoven into her healing process.

During this period of her life, Elena discovered that processing the grief and coming to terms with it was just as important as letting go of it in order to go on and build a stronger, more self-aware life. Her friends served as her rock, reassuring her that even though the night could be long, daylight would eventually arrive with their unwavering support and sometimes jokes.

Between the regular highs and lows that characterised Elena's existence, there were times when she experienced nights that were unlike any other nights, full of excitement and unrestrained adventure. These were moments that disrupted the pattern. The real vibrancy of her relationships with Elodie, Mike, and Rachel were evident in these unplanned adventures, which were set against the backdrop of her daily problems. Because of their enduring faith in one another, these events became priceless memories that highlighted exciting and colourful moments in Elena's life, making it stand out from the more sombre sections.

On certain evenings when everything appeared excessively motionless and silent, Elena would sense the nagging sense of adventure nagging at her heart. These were the nights when the moon was more than just a celestial body in the sky; it was a beacon that guided her to discover the pleasures concealed beneath the veil of obscurity. She would go through the property's silent corridors with the dexterity of an experienced escape artist, each step a sign of the excitement of soon-to-be liberated. The warden, not knowing of the nighttime mischievous activities taking place under their supervision, slept on.

The world gasped as Elena sneaked past the guards and arrived outside, where Elodie was waiting with a smile that promised more adventures. Their meeting was a whispered agreement to rebel against the ordinary, a secret between two souls bound by friendship. As a reminder of the impenetrable circle they built, Mike and Rachel would be waiting for them as they ventured into the night together.

The city turned into their playground with its neon lights and hushed promises. The beat of liberation pulsed through nightclubs, with every song calling out to the inner wildness that each person carried. Elodie and Rachel, who embody joy and abandonment, would find comfort in the dance, as their moves celebrated the present. At some point, Mike and Elena would join the dance, their inhibitions melting to the beat of the night, while they were equipped with shots of alcohol that burnt trails of courage down their throats.

Even though they were infrequent, these excursions served as benchmarks for Elena as she mapped out her recovery. If only temporarily, the shadows that lurked in the recesses of her heart were banished when she was with her friends. She was able to navigate the darkness that had once threatened to engulf her because to the trust that served as the foundation of their friendship.

When the quiet of her own company became too much on certain days, Elena sought solace in Rachel and Elodie's houses. In Rachel's home, the hours would pass in a whirl of chatter and company. It was a place of warmth and joy. Their nights were spent glowing from shared dreams and secrets, which served as a reminder of the connection that bound their spirits together.

However, Elena discovered a kinship that extended beyond into the domains of comprehension and acceptance with Elodie. In addition to being a physical location, Elodie's house served as an emotional haven where Elena felt free to open up about her past traumas without worrying about being judged. Their late-night journeys were explorations of uncharted territory, with the city streets serving as a background for their hushed assurances. The environment beyond their car's windows was a jumble of lights and shadows, reflecting the intricacies of their feelings and ideas.

They developed a ritual of watching films and eating snacks late at night; it was a simple pleasure that embodied their connection. Elena and Elodie would lose themselves in stories that reflected their own experiences in the soft glow of the television, with the taste of popcorn still on their tongues. Each movie served as a mirror of the journey they were on.

Through these events, both monumental and insignificant, Elena started to create a new story about herself, one in which the suffering of the past was accepted but did not come to define who she was. She was a living example of the strength of friendship—a force so potent that it could lift the curtain of darkness that had obscured her vision—because she trusted Elodie, Mike, and Rachel.

Elena found laughter and joy again in their companionship, as well as the strength that comes from knowing you are not alone. Every experience, every moment of stillness together, every burst of laughter in the middle of the night was a step closer to her recovery. The world, which had previously been a desolate place, has changed to one full with opportunity and promise.

Elena carried these lessons with her throughout her life—love, grief, and the healing power of friendship. She now realised that even while life may have unhappy endings to some of its chapters, experiences and the people we travel with enrich the narrative as it unfolds. Elena faced every day knowing that Elodie, Mike, and Rachel would be there to support her. She was excited about the adventures that lay ahead and felt comforted in the idea that she would never have to face anything alone in the future.

Though Elena's journey was far from finished, the person who arrived in Durban—driven by optimism and a desire for resolution—was no longer Elena. Day by day, she was becoming a person who could find happiness in the quiet company of her own soul as well as in the company of others. Although there was still uncertainty in her path, Elena was prepared for it since she had the knowledge gained by spending time alone with friends and reflecting on her life.

Chapter - 27
Digital Heartstrings: Elena's Quest for Connection

While navigating the maze of academic life, Elena found comfort in Elodie's companionship; her lively personality and steadfast encouragement had been a lighthouse throughout her darkest moments. Amidst the vibrant atmosphere of academics, their friendship had grown and developed into a beautiful tapestry made of secrets and laughter. A glimmer of excitement appeared in Elodie's eyes as she confided in Elena about Kian, a new chapter in her life that appeared to hold the happiness she so rightly deserved, during one of their leisurely strolls about the university grounds.

Elena, who has always been a helpful friend, was overjoyed to hear the news. She perceived Elodie's joy as a reflection of what might be possible when the past heartbreaks faded. The ease with which encouragement was exchanged between them demonstrated the strength of their relationship. It seemed as though the cosmos was working together to weave love into Elodie and Kian's lives as their romance took off overnight.

Elodie's newfound love was slowly blossoming over the course of a week, with each day disclosing a flower. Elodie announced that she was excited to present Elena to Kian at that moment, but she was also apprehensive about it. Elena nodded, fascinated by this new man who had won her friend over. However, she couldn't help but observe Elodie's unwillingness to discuss how they first met. Elena received a mosaic of humorous half-answers to each question that was skillfully avoided.

Looking pleasant in the midday light, the day of the introduction finally arrived. After Elodie's confession, Elena had been drawn to mysteries, and now she sat across from Kian, the embodiment of one. Before they arrived at the entrance of Elena's previous connection with Peter, their conversation meandered through the hallways of offbeat subjects. Her memories behind the door were a mixture of happiness and sadness. She opened it with caution.

Kian brought up the topic of going forward with a kind push. Even though his remarks came as a surprise, they struck a chord with Elena since it was a truth that she was gradually coming to. There was a combination of surprise and reflection when it was suggested to use a dating app to discover new places. A dash of reality was added to Kian's advice when he disclosed that Elodie and his paths had crossed on the dating app. Elena couldn't help but find Elodie's modest response endearing; it was a ballet of shyness and happiness that depicted a modern version of love.

In the days that followed, Elena was at a loss for what to do. The counsel of a recently met person made her consider the path she had taken towards healing and self-discovery. It was terrifying and thrilling to think that she would let new people into her heart. It was a bold move that demanded faith to venture into the uncharted territory of dating in the digital age.

With Elodie's success as motivation and Kian's gentle encouragement, Elena cautiously delved into the dating app world, considering each swipe as a query and each match as a possible response. The procedure involved striking a balance between the need for friendship and the dread of being vulnerable, creating a patchwork of hope and hesitation. But in this virtual dance, Elena unearthed aspects of herself that had been hidden in the fallout from her romance with Peter.

Not only was the journey to find a new partner, but it was also an attempt to rediscover Elena, to validate her value, and to show that she was ready to accept love once more. It had to do with accepting the wounds from the past while letting herself dream of a future filled with happiness and hope.

Elena's friendships with Elodie and Kian developed into a fabric of encouragement, teasing, and life experiences as she moved through this new phase. They turned into mirrors, each reflecting the personal development, struggles, and triumphs they had experienced. Elodie's connection with Kian, which grew out of a chance online meeting, served as a warning about the erratic nature of love.

During this journey, Elena discovered that moving on was an homage to the heart's ability to heal and fall in love again rather than a betrayal of prior loves. Once only an idea, the dating app evolved into a doorway to an endless array of opportunities, with each match taking a step forward and away from the shadows of their pasts into the light of their prospective futures.

The tale of Elena, Elodie, and Kian is proof of the strength of friendship, the resiliency of the human heart, and the bravery required to let love into one's life once more. It's a story that skillfully combines the complexity of love, the anguish of parting ways, and the beauty of fresh starts. With eyes wide open to the promise of tomorrow and a heart strengthened by the lessons of the past, Elena writes her story onward.

Elena set off on a path of recovery and self-discovery when she entered the dating app world, a virtual space full of opportunities and the draw of making new friends. Her tentative strides forward were evidenced by every notification and "like" she received. Her profile served as a canvas on which she painted the subtleties of her personality and her aspirations for the future. As the app brought strangers into her daily existence, the city, with its multitude of individuals seeking company, felt suddenly both huge and intimate.

Elena saw a mosaic of faces and tales as she scrolled through the profiles, each one looking for something that spoke to their own ambitions. First conversations were usually circumspect, a tango of salutations and little talk. The anonymity provided a certain level of comfort, acting as a shield against the fragility of fresh starts. But as time carved out its inexorable course, Elena discovered that she was lured into more in-depth discussions with a few people, their words serving as a bridge over the digital barrier.

But the idea of actually getting together remained a barrier she was reluctant to overcome. Text on a screen offered a safe haven and authority over the development and complexity of these emerging relationships. The well-curated personas provided by the strangers behind the profiles continued to be mysteries, masking their true objectives. Elena's caution served as a shield, built by the knowledge gained from her trip thus far and the lingering effects of prior injuries.

Elena was pushed towards accepting her first in-person meeting by curiosity and the need for company, despite her misgivings. The outing was portrayed as a casual get-together, complete with a movie and dinner together rather than as a date. It was a set-up that provided structure and allowed for natural conversation, a test of compatibility outside of chat rooms.

Elena entered the mall with a mixture of excitement and trepidation. Her attire inhabited the space between casual and well-chosen attire. As she approached the prearranged meeting place, the bustling hallways, with their cacophony of shoppers and far-off chatter, seemed to abruptly go quiet. With a welcoming smile on his lips, the boy who had only been a face in the pixels of her phone screen had come to life.

Selecting the film based on its objectivity provided a haven of shadows and mutual attention, a release from the examination of first perceptions.

However, Elena sensed a discordant undertone as the credits rolled and they arrived at the lunch location—a subtle realisation that the potential connection they had previously discussed via text fell flat when they met in person. All in all, it was a nice talk that stayed just on the safe side of generalisations and courteous questions, avoiding true interest altogether.

The eagerness that had greeted Elena's preparations for the day gradually subsided as the hours passed, to be replaced by a certainty that this encounter would not inspire any more research. Although the boy was friendly and interesting, he failed to arouse in Elena the emotions she had hoped to rekindle—the excitement of a relationship that held promise for more, the gut feeling that revealed possibilities.

Resolved based on the lack of chemistry between them rather than the obvious flaw, she silently decided not to pursue anything further with him. It represented an appreciation for the intricate web of human connection and an awareness that not every encounter would lead to a more meaningful one.

Though not what she had anticipated, there were still valuable lessons to be learned from the event. Elena found solace in the idea that patience is crucial, and that she should allow herself the freedom to make connections without worrying about results right away. It brought home to her the importance of spending time alone yourself, the serenity that comes from being alone, and the fact that finding the right person to connect with on a deep level was a journey that required time and patience.

Not just for the encounter that day, but also for this stage of the experiment, Elena felt a feeling of closure as she left the mall. With its limitless potential, the dating app stayed on her phone, serving as a window into other lives. Elena, however, approached it with a fresh outlook, one that was informed by experience and the understanding that the appropriate connections would emerge in their own time.

Elena continued to use dating apps in the ensuing weeks and months, approaching them with a mixture of caution and curiosity. She had discussions, laughed with and gained insight from others, and sometimes she even went to in-person gatherings. Every conversation she had was a strand in the ever-widening tapestry of her life, woven together by the desire to meet someone who would complete her.

The relationships that had helped Elena get through her worst moments and the self-improvement she had cultivated kept her grounded throughout it all. It wasn't an easy road, but the process of letting go of Peter and opening up to the possibility of fresh starts was full with opportunities to learn about herself, about love, and about the myriad undiscovered tales that waited for her in the future.

Elena had experimented with the digital dating app world, which offered the possibility of fresh starts and the ability to alter her narrative, as a result of her tortuous path through the healing and self-discovery processes. Amidst the several meetings and brief discussions, one particular match caught her attention—a boy whose early interactions exuded a hint of promise, a resonance that seemed appealing enough to investigate further than words on a screen.

The idea of meeting was suggested after a fortnight of messaging during which time they cautiously danced to get to know one another. By offering to pick Elena up after her courses, the boy demonstrated his awareness of the routines of university life and helped to close the distance between their virtual and real worlds. With a hopeful sense of anticipation, Elena nodded and her pulse began to race at the thought of what this new chapter might hold.

Although the day of their encounter was filled with the typical commotion of student life, Elena sensed that it was also fraught with the potential. An important turning point in her journey occurred as she got into his car and left the comfortable confines of her university to venture into the uncharted area of a real-world encounter.

They met at a cosy cafe that provided a cosy setting for their first encounter. Their discussion became less awkward as they shared experiences and ordered pizzas, which was a clue that things would get better. But the afternoon took a surprising turn when they withdrew to the car in search of a private, peaceful place to resume their conversation.

There was hesitancy as the boy tried to kiss Elena, an unspoken but highly suggestive gesture. Elena declined to respond because she was torn between the need for a relationship and the integrity of her own space. Her reply was one of preservation rather than rejection, a tacit declaration of her ease and speed in the developing story of their friendship.

He made several attempts, but each time was met with the same indirect rejection, which raised a question of comfort, which Elena skillfully avoided by shifting the subject or using a subtle combination of politeness and confidence. However, in response to his persistent approaches, a part of her wondered if returning the favour may open up a new dimension to their interaction, a test of her own willingness to face the ghosts of her past.

It was entirely up to her whether or not to return the kiss, an indecisive moment of self-discovery as she worked to define her boundaries and wants. The brief kisses that followed were heavy with a lot of unanswered questions and doubts about what she wanted and what she was willing to open herself to.

On the other hand, Elena was experiencing a whirlwind of emotions as night fell over the activities of the previous day. Her first sentiments of ambivalence gave way to a deep sense of unease as she realised that their physical intimacy was a moment sparked by curiosity and possibly a misguided need to prove something to herself rather than a true representation of connection.

Elena was uncomfortable and reluctant to continue interacting with the boy when he extended polite invites to meet again. She was still figuring out the complex dance of healing and self-discovery, as seen by the contradiction between her actions and her feelings, which she was not ready to bridge.

Elena turned to Mike, a source of support and comprehension in her life, in her quest for closure. Mike became the go-between, a voice of understanding and clarity thanks to his constant support. His exchange with the boy was a nuanced mix of stern insistence that Elena needed time and space, and respect for her path. Mike's intervention was more than just a show of friendship; it was evidence of the strong tie between them, one that valued Elena's independence and her process of working with the fallout from her previous relationship.

Thinking back on the interaction and its consequences, Elena saw it as a new phase in her path and a lesson in the value of following her gut instincts and being true to her emotions. Although disconcerting, the experience served as a reminder of the value of self-compassion and the fact that the road to healing was one that included both periods of clarity and confusion.

Elena took comfort in her friends' company in the days that followed, as well as in the talks and laughter that filled her days and the reflective quiet of her evenings. Every action she took and every choice she made contributed to the narrative of her changing life, one that praised her fortitude, her ability to reflect on herself, and her unwavering hope for a time when respect and love were mutually exclusive.

A reminder of the complexity of the human heart was provided by Elena's trip, which was replete with both strong and vulnerable times. That served as a monument to the strength of friendship, the value of personal space, and the bravery needed to forge forth into uncharted territory. Elena had a stronger sense of her own value, a heart that was open to the possibilities of love, and a spirit that was unwavering in the face of life's erratic swings as she continued to forge her path through the terrain of her existence.

Chapter - 28
Elena's Realization and Retreat

Elena's ongoing exploration of the dating app environment is evidence of her determined desire to keep going and make new friends. She persisted in her quest for self-discovery despite the obstacles and times when she felt doubtful about herself, moving forward from the memories of her previous relationship with each app swipe. There were a lot of opportunities in this universe, some short-lived and some hinting at something longer-term.

During one such trip, Elena decided to get together with a boy who had caught her curiosity among the sea of profiles. Their internet communication had been a back-and-forth interaction that suggested mutual understanding and curiosity, and it had flowed easily. This initial connection gave her confidence to agree to a face-to-face meeting, which was a leap of faith into the unknown which is in person engagement.

They decided to meet at a nice, quiet pub where the sound of chattering voices and glasses clinking would not distract from their private discourse. They laughed and told incidents as they discussed the stories of their lives over a glass of beer. But as the night wore on, it was clear that the spark in their letters that had appeared so promising was absent from reality. Though enjoyable, Elena came to the realisation that the encounter lacked the chemistry and depth she had been longing for, and it left her feeling quietly decided.

There was a friendly parting, a shared realisation that certain relationships are destined to be transient even with the greatest of intentions. There was only the silent recognition of a shared and gone moment; there was no resentment or feeling of sorrow. Both parties agreed in silence to continue their own quests for connection, and in the days that followed, there was no more communication from either side.

Unbothered, Elena continued her search and discovered a new match and opportunity to make a real connection. This time, they chose to watch a movie together, allowing them to enjoy an experience side by side and assess their chemistry through silent glances and hushed conversations in the dark theatre.

With her pulse pounding from excitement, Elena sat in the dimly lit theatre. For the last thirty minutes or so, she had been flirting with this boy, whose name she did not even know. In addition to buying her drink and popcorn, he had also been whispering filthy jokes in her ear. Particularly in this public setting, Elena couldn't believe how turned-on she was becoming.

Elena was compelled to slant closer to the boy as the film got underway. She nestled onto his chest as he wrapped his arm around her. His fingers moved slowly down to her chest, stroking her breast through her clothes. His fingers caressed her tender nipples, causing Elena to experience a surge of pleasure throughout her body.

They met eyes as she raised her head to gaze at him. He leaned forward and kissed her deeply without thinking twice. The dance of their tongues together had Elena's heart racing. Her need for him to stop growing stronger, as she was becoming increasingly erotic.

The boy's hand showed more adventure as the movie went on. With deliberate movement, he moved his hand beneath her dress and down her chest, placing his fingertips squarely on her chest. Though Elena gasped a little, she did not intervene. He was giving her so much pleasure that she was getting engrossed in the moment and lost in it.

Now resting on her stomach, the boy's hand made its way down her body. As his fingers drew nearer to her panties, Elena's heart began to race in her chest. She bit her lip and closed her eyes, waiting to see what he would do.

She was startled when she felt his hand move under her pants and begin to massage her clit. Elena moaned quietly, not wanting to be the centre of attention in the packed theatre. With his skilful finger movements against her tender spot, the boy appeared indifferent to her presence.

Elena's moans got louder and more frequent as the film went on. She could feel herself drawing further and nearer to the edge as the boy's fingers continued to glide. She couldn't believe how simple it was for him to make her feel this way because she was so turned on.

The boy then took an unexpected action. Grasping Elena's palm, he laid it against his pants, on his already hard and dripping dick. Elena did not back down, even as her eyes grew wide with shock. She was compelled to touch his erection because she could feel the heat coming from it.

She felt his dick get more harder as she softly touched it through his trousers. Elena felt a wave of strength come over her when the youngster let out a low groan. It was her who was giving him this feeling, and it was immensely pleasurable.

The boy wasn't finished, though. He took Elena's hand and carefully pulled it inside his trousers. She was amazed at how much she wanted him, especially when she felt his hard, moist dick in her fingers. She began to mimic the motion of his fingers on her clit by moving her hand up and down.

Elena felt a surge of clarity sweep over her as the moment grew more intense and she realised she was about to have a very personal experience. She pulled back her hands and pushed him away, a firm action that demonstrated her independence and comfort level and revealed her immediate understanding of her own limits and wishes. This gesture was a declaration of her own demands and boundaries as much as the physical distance between them. For Elena, it was a moment of empowerment, a resounding declaration that her comfort and permission came first, reaffirming her right to control the direction and speed of her interactions.

A sense of remorse and contempt passed over Elena as she and the lad left the movie theatre. She was incredibly uneasy about whatever had happened in the dark of the movie theatre. Hurrying to the washroom, she was overcome with nausea, a physical manifestation of her emotional turmoil, leading her to vomit. The encounter served as a sharp reminder of how unpredictable and occasionally uncomfortable it can be to push outside of one's comfort zone, particularly when seeking out new relationships. Elena made the snap decision to cut ties with the boy and blocked him on her phone. Her quick response was her taking back control and was essential to getting over the bad experience so she could carry on with her adventure with a strengthened sense of caution and self-respect.

Elena decided to block the boy after having a flash of insight driven by a combination of disappointment and a strong desire to keep herself safe. It was a final move, a boundary established not out of spite but rather out of a newly discovered respect for her own emotional terrain. Even while it seemed harsh, she was exercising her right to free will by refusing to do what didn't feel right and to go forward with her trip at her own pace.

Despite some depressing occasions, Elena's experiences weren't in vain. Every interaction, every choice to stick together or go separate ways, was a milestone on her path to self-discovery. These lessons helped her realise how valuable she was and that finding connection involves learning about oneself just as much as it does about finding someone.

Elena discovered comfort in her own company and strength in accepting the detours her journey took her down in the loneliness that followed. She realised that finding love and friendship is a difficult journey full of ups and downs, and that every move she made, every swipe she made, every encounter she had was a part of the complex dance that is life.

She fell into a cycle of trial and error when it came to meeting boys in an attempt to find a spark that might turn into something more. The goal of every date was to discover a kindred spirit whose vibrations matched her own by attempting to peel back the layers of strangers' identities. It was a search for comprehension and affinities, for the elusive chemistry that held promise.

After a long and confusing online dating experience, the date with the boy who finally seemed to resonate with her was a ray of optimism. Their first meeting had been full with promise, the kind of relationship Elena had been longing for. Motivated by their mutual suitability, she asked him out on another date, taking the investigation of this developing relationship one step further. The supper they had together was an extension of their bond; it was an intimate and thrilling event. As he drove her home, Elena permitted herself to think that maybe, just maybe, this time, things might turn out differently.

But soon enough, the ugly truth of online dating emerged. Like Elena had done on past dates, the male decided to cut off their connection suddenly and blocked her without giving any prior notice. Elena was left with a range of complicated feelings by this deed, which was a reflection of her own previous choices. She had hoped to avoid the usual pain of rejection this time, but there sit was, stinging her. However, there was also an acknowledgement of her own actions, a realisation that she had also travelled the same path—one marked by temporary ties and abrupt endings.

After stepping away from the digital dating scene, Elena's resolve wavered one evening, leading her back to the familiar glow of her phone's screen. It was there that she met another boy, and she connected with him instantly and completely. They soon found they had a passion for independent movies and were exchanging amusing and sincere texts. They agreed to watch films together for the evening, seizing the opportunity.

Elena was thrilled to be staying at the boy's home for the night. The boy gave her a passionate kiss as soon as she got there. He took her by surprise, and Elena couldn't help but fall into his arms.

On the couch, they cuddled together as the movie began. Elena was feeling cold all over as the boy's hand ran through her hair and down her back. His touch had mesmerised her, and she was eager to see what was going to happen next.

The boy turned to Elena and abruptly stopped the movie. He leaned forward without saying anything, giving her another, deeper kiss. Her heart began to race and her body began to ache for more as soon as Elena felt it. He touched her shoulders and then her back, drawing her in closer.

The boy began to take off his t-shirt to display his toned body as the kiss went on. Elena's gaze followed his abs and chest as she couldn't help but appreciate him. After that, he turned to face her and motioned for her to take off her t-shirt. Elena hesitated at first, but she gave in to the boy's alluring stare and his touch on her exposed flesh. She let him take off her t-shirt so he could see her lace bra.

Elena felt the boy's hands graze every part of her body. Then he reached behind her and removed her bra, exposing her full set of breasts. He began licking and squeezing them right away since he was unable to resist. Elena let out a sigh of delight, her body burning with passion.

Elena was shocked at how turned on she was as they kept making out. They didn't intend to have sex because they didn't have any condoms. However, the boy then took Elena's hand and slipped it into his pants, exposing his erection, which was stiff and pounding. Elena was unable to resist when he asked her to play with it. She put her hand around it and began to stroke it, enjoying the sensation of the hardness and heat.

The boy then reached into her pants, but Elena flinched. Since she didn't want to take a chance, she knew they had no protection. But the boy persisted, and with his seductive skills, he succeeded in getting her jeans off and her legs wide. Now when she was just wearing her panties, Elena wouldn't allow him to take them off.

Unwilling to be stopped, the boy ripped her panties apart, exposing her very wet and aching pussy. Elena felt so hot that it was unbelievable, and her body was aching for more. She felt waves of ecstasy go through her body as the boy began massaging her clit. She let out a loud moan, losing herself in the experience.

The boy collapsed on her and began kissing and sucking her pussy, unable to contain his adoration. Elena's body was shaking with pleasure; she was in a state of euphoria. Though she was aware that it wasn't safe, all she wanted was to have sex with him.

Elena realised what was happening and stopped the boy just before he could enter her. He was reminded that they were defenceless by her yelling at him. Recognising his error, the boy gave her a heartfelt apology and embrace.

They both dressed and prepared for bed after a while. However, there was no denying the tension between them. How close they had come to having sex without protection was something Elena couldn't stop thinking about. She felt disappointed but also relieved.

Elena's reflections were further strengthened by her next contact with this boy, which resulted in a night spent together. The daybreak was accompanied by a wash of disgust and sorrow, notwithstanding the initial excitement of mischievous behaviour. The night's events, which had before been clouded by the moment's excitement, now appeared hollow and reflected the emptiness that these fleeting encounters frequently left behind.

Elena's life took a radical shift with this epiphany. She realised that her inner desire for real companionship was not being satisfied by the cycle of meetings and partings, of looking for approval and connection via the prism of a dating app. Not only did blocking the boy from the previous night signal the end of another brief encounter, but it also marked the symbolic end of her online dating journey.

Elena decided to stop using dating apps as a means of preserving and upholding her dignity. It was an admission that relationships worth having will emerge in their own time and manner and that the road to finding a fit spouse could not be hurried or forced. With this choice, Elena entered a new stage of her journey in which she decided to put her own happiness and growth ahead of the approval of love relationships.

Elena continued her trip and came to the realisation that the huge world of online dating, with its attraction of seemingly endless alternatives, was not the right path for her. Through the highs and lows of temporary relationships, she developed a deep sense of self-awareness and clarity on her true desires. Elena made a different decision, deciding to distance herself from the fleeting world of dating apps and the fragile connections they promoted. She now realised that her deeper yearning for real, enduring relationships could not be satisfied by the fleeting interactions she encountered online. Armed with this knowledge, she abandoned the virtual search for friendship and instead embraced the depth of self-

development and the hunt for real, meaningful relationships that go beyond screens.

Elena's narrative illustrates the difficulties associated with modern dating; it is a story of optimism, disappointment, and the search for something deeper. It serves as a reminder that although the heart may travel in search of companionship, the most meaningful relationships frequently emerge from the most unexpected places—that is, from the unpredictable, wandering routes of life rather than from the well-planned algorithms of dating apps.

Chapter - 29
Beyond University Walls: Journeys of Friendship and Futures

Elena's life story is a dynamic one, and her experiences using digital dating turned out to be a turning point that led her to find solace in friendship. The companionship of Elena's friends, a group that had grown to be her anchor in the choppy waters of self-discovery and healing, provided her with comfort as the dust fell on her trials with transient connections. Even though she had failed to find a feeling of belonging in her love endeavours, Mike, Rachel, and Elodie had all individually weaved themselves into the fabric of her life.

Elodie, the true local of Pretoria, emerged as the sister of Elena's soul. Their relationship went beyond the typical boundaries of friendship because of their common experiences and unstated understandings. Elodie was the one who had supported Elena during her highs and lows; her persistent presence served as a constant reminder of the unflinching support that friends could offer. Elena saw in Elodie not simply a companion but also a mirror of her hopes, anxieties, and pleasures.

Mike, however, had changed from being just a passing acquaintance to becoming a constant source of support in Elena's life. She found solace in his company and direction in his wisdom as she made her way through the maze of her feelings. Their friendship was deep and light-hearted at the same time, allowing Elena to be herself without fear of being seen as authentic.

Although Rachel was close to Elena at first, she had progressively grown to be known as someone who was on the outside of Elena's inner circle. Their friendship had changed, becoming less close but still very much flavoured with respect for one another and their shared history from their early college years.

Having grown out of their shared experiences of college life, Kian and Elodie's love is a unique success story that began with a swipe of a dating app. Despite the often fleeting connections formed on such platforms, they found themselves among the fortunate few for whom digital sparks translated into a lasting bond. Had it not been for their coincidental internet match, the two university students' paths might have never intersected. They recognised the peculiarity of their circumstances and were appreciative of the fortunate meeting that developed into a bond based on common goals, difficulties, and the innumerable little moments that characterise college life. They were not unaware of this turn of events.

Elena's days were filled with a spirit of adventure, camaraderie, and respect for one another because of the intricate web of events that Elodie, Mike, Elena, and Elodie's partner, Kian, knitted together. Their travels together, which included impromptu drives through the vibrant landscapes of Pretoria and peaceful afternoons spent watching sunsets, served as pauses on Elena's journey to realising the meaning and fulfilment of friendship.

Their shared rides, when the world seemed to open up in front of them with endless possibilities, were the ideal match for Elena's passion for automobiles and the excitement of the open road. These adventures were proof of the freedom and happiness that friendship could bring, whether they were undertaken to chase the last light of the day or to discover new places. Here, the only things present were the open road, the company of friends, and the mutual joy of discovery—there were no demands or expectations.

Elena loved their evenings spent dining outside under the sky, their words flowing as freely as the wine. She felt at ease here, in the middle of the chuckles and glass clinking, something she had not felt in a long time. Her soul was soothed by these get-togethers' effortlessness and lack of pretence or impressing others, which served as a reminder of the basic pleasures in life.

Every trip became a journey into the heart of friendship for Elena, and her vacations with this close-knit group became her favourite times of the year. Unrestrained happiness, memories formed and experiences exchanged, and relationships reinforced by the shared struggles and victories of travel characterised these times. Every experience they had was a strand in the intricate fabric of their shared tale, whether it involved overcoming the difficulties of a new city or discovering happiness in the peace of the outdoors.

Their friendship was an influential influence within the university. Projects they worked on together demonstrated their combined creativity and intelligence, a synthesis of viewpoints that frequently produced amazing results. Elena discovered a new aspect of her friendships through her academic endeavours: a cooperative attitude that provided inspiration and drive.

Elena had a breakthrough when she realised that friends may replace the voids left by her longing for romantic love. She discovered a different yet no less profound kind of love in Mike, Rachel, Elodie, and Kian—a love based on respect for one another, understanding, and the ability to be who one truly is. Here, there were no hidden conflicts or expectations, nor were there any physical expectations. Elena could put her past behind her and welcome the present with open arms because of their friendship, which served as a haven.

Elevated by the unwavering light of friendship, this period of Elena's life served as evidence of the transformational potential of platonic love. The statement emphasised the reality that, on occasion, the strongest bonds are not created during intense romantic moments but rather throughout the shared experience of life's ups and downs, joys and sorrows. Regardless of the path Elena chose, she would never have to walk it alone, so she looked forward with a heart strengthened by that knowing. Friendships served as her compass, pointing her in the direction of uncharted territory and a future where joy and serenity would not only exist but also be permanently nourished by the enduring links of friendship.

A tangible sense of uncertainty started to permeate Elena and her close-knit group of friends' everyday interactions as the last year of college unfolded its chances and challenges. Their scholastic adventure was coming to an end, which meant that decisions regarding the future were looming huge on the horizon. It was a sign of transition. Mike, Kian, Elodie, and Elena found themselves at a crossroads in this crucible of transformation, each driven in a different direction by their hopes, concerns, and dreams for what waited outside the university's doors.

Mike, whose heart was still bound to his hometown by a distant relationship, believed that the job market held the key to his future. He had learned the value of consistency and the necessity of laying the groundwork for a future in which he and his partner could both be supported by it from a distance. His practicality acted as a stabilising influence, reminding his companions of the things that were really important by the time college ended.

As someone who shared Mike's goal, Kian was likewise lured to the quick satisfaction that comes with starting a job. He was well aware that the trials of the outside world would put their relationship to the true test, even if his connection with Elodie had grown in the supportive environment of their university. Working would allow him to become independent and better able to provide for his loved ones and himself. It was more than simply a means to an end.

Elodie and Elena, however, were not prepared to give up the world of academia. They both had a strong desire to learn more and pursue higher education since they thought that education had the ability to broaden perspectives and open doors. After completing her undergraduate studies, Elodie saw additional coursework as a means of expanding her knowledge in her field of study and strengthening the groundwork she had already established. Driven by her own drive for personal growth and by Elodie's enthusiasm, Elena saw pursuing higher education as a way to reinvent herself, build on the knowledge she had gained from the past, and create a future that was uniquely her own.

While each member was engaged in private discussions, the group as a whole was focused on completing a major project that served as the capstone of their academic pursuits. This project was more than simply an assignment; it was a representation of their journey together and a capstone project that captured the spirit of their friendship and shared experiences. It was a monument to their joint intellect, creativity, and hard work.

Focus, teamwork, and a steadfast dedication to excellence were required for the project. Their days were characterised by continual idea sharing, brainstorming sessions, and late-night study sessions. There was a lot on the line, since their grades would determine not just their senior year outcomes but also their future prospects.

The buddies found themselves having more in-depth discussions about their particular goals and the paths they were thinking about as they worked through the challenges of their project. These conversations were exciting because of the possibilities even though they were tinged with fear of the unknown. They served as a reminder that, in spite of the many paths they could choose, the friendships they had made while attending college would always be there to support and encourage one another.

Even though the endeavour was difficult, it also acted as a diversion from the impending uncertainties of the future. Their mutual aim, which required them to complement each other's shortcomings and capitalise on each other's strengths, was the shared endeavour that brought them closer. The procedure was a miniature version of the actual world, where cooperation, understanding, and respect for one another were essential for success.

The realisation that they would soon be apart grew stronger as the project got closer to completion. The comforts and rituals of college life, together with the warmth of companionship, were about to give way to the pressures of the outside world. Elodie and Elena, with their dreams of going back to school, and Mike and Kian, with their intentions to start a career, were ready to set out on adventures that would put their friendship to the test.

Nevertheless, despite all of this uncertainty, there was also hope, a conviction that the relationships they had created would stand the test of time and space. Their friendship served as a monument to the enduring power of connection, strengthened by the experiences they had in common and the obstacles they had surmounted as a team. It served as a reminder that, wherever life may lead them, they would always have a foundation of recollections and a common past that would bind them together.

Thus, the final project served as more than simply a report card; it represented their group's journey and served as a link between the past and the future. They knew that when they put their everything into finishing it, it would mark the close of one chapter and the start of a new one. Elena, Mike, Kian, and Elodie discovered not only the pinnacle of their academic careers but also a springboard for the adventures that awaited them in this transitional area between the known and the unknown.

A reminder that every farewell holds the possibility of a new hello is provided by their story, which is a tapestry of friendship, ambition, and the bittersweet truth of transition. It was certain that the relationships they had built would serve as a compass to help them navigate the unknown waters of life beyond college, even as they stood on the precipice of the future, each with their own hopes and worries.

For Elena and her close friends, the completion of their final project was a major turning point that came about as a result of months of perseverance, commitment, and teamwork. The excellent scores they earned demonstrated their achievement, but it was also a bittersweet occasion, a sign of the changes that were soon to reverberate throughout their close-knit community. While they were happy with their academic performance, they were also aware that this victory marked the end of an era and the start of new pathways that would put their relationship's sturdiness to the test.

Following graduation, Kian and Mike found themselves drawn from the comforts of Pretoria to the exciting and bustling city of Cape Town by a plethora of potential options. Throughout their time at university, Kian and Elodie's friendship grew closer, and now Kian was joining a rapidly growing startup in a senior role. Although the position was a dream come true and gave him the opportunity to demonstrate his abilities in the cutthroat world of business, it came at a high cost: he would have to be away from Elodie.

Mike's career path diverged slightly as a result of his abilities and diligence in landing a coveted position in a well-known corporation. He could start his career on a great scale and the position was a testimonial to his ability, but it also meant he would have to say goodbye to the deep friendship he had developed with Kian, Elodie, and Elena. Though it came with the burden of having to say goodbye to his friends who had grown to be his second family, the relocation to Cape Town was an acceptance of the difficulties and opportunities for growth that lay ahead.

Elodie and Elena, who were left behind in Pretoria, had their own difficulties. It was not an easy choice to decide to take a year off in order to study for entrance tests into internationally recognised universities. It was a calculated decision motivated by ambition and a desire to continue their study, but it also meant having to live without Kian and Mike, whose company had been a regular source of encouragement and friendship.

The pang of separation was particularly painful for Elodie. Her bond with Kian had grown into something more than just a relationship; it was a source of happiness and security for her. The distance that separated them now was a formidable challenge that would try their resolve and strengthen their relationship. A poignant reminder of what they had and what they were striving to keep, the quiet moments they had spent, the laughter and dreams that had woven them closer, now rang in her memory.

With Mike starting his new path, Elena experienced a similar sense of loss. A fundamental aspect of her time at university had been their friendship, which was based on respect, common experiences, and a profound comprehension of each other's advantages and disadvantages. There is a gap where Mike's humour, wisdom, and steadfast support formerly resided due to his departure.

Their discussions served as a lifeline that kept the group together despite their physical separation from one another and between Pretoria and Cape Town. They cheered each other on in times of doubt and loneliness, gave updates on their progress, and offered support to one another. Elodie and Elena had a plan to get back together after finishing their exam prep, which gave them optimism that they would eventually get together again, even if it was just for a short while before they went off on their own paths.

There was a huge gap left by Kian and Mike's absence while Elodie and Elena focused on their academics. The significance of their personal goals and the visions they were putting in endless effort to realise were also brought to light by it. A major motivator that kept them concentrated and inspired over the long hours of preparation was the idea of studying overseas, of broadening their perspectives and seizing new chances.

Notwithstanding their differences in geography and career choices, the friendship amongst the four friends held strong. It demonstrated how deeply they were connected, a bond that had been reinforced by the difficulties they had overcome together and developed in the harsh environment of academic life. The basis they continued to build upon while they managed the intricacies of their changing lives was their shared past, the recollections of late-night study sessions, entertaining excursions, and meaningful chats.

Their excitement about getting back together did not diminish over time. Anticipating to share the same place once more, they hung onto the hope of being a beacon in the shadows and looked forward to the end of the year. Enjoying the comfort of each other's company and sharing stories of their exploits was what they looked forward to. Their trip was a mirror of their development, resiliency, and the unshakable link of their friendship as they went from being college students to people forging their own lives. Their bond acted as an anchor in the midst of shifting circumstances and unpredictability, a continual reminder that they would always have a place in each other's hearts no matter where life took them.

Chapter - 30
Abroad Beginnings: From Homeland to Hamburg, Germany

Elena and Elodie's life paths had led them through a maze of obstacles, chances, and unrelenting study for the tests that served as barriers to their goals for the future. Working together, they overcame the challenges of their academic pursuits, complementing their studies with worthwhile classes that expanded their perspectives and enhanced their understanding. As a result of their unrelenting drive and support for one another, their friendship grew stronger during this hard period of study, which was characterised by late-night study sessions and a shared sense of concern about approaching tests.

Elena and Elodie reached their separate exam centres with a mixture of resolution and trepidation on the day of the exams. It was finally here—the culmination of months of effort and commitment—a pivotal moment that would determine their future trajectories. Each question they answered seemed to resound with the weight of their aspirations and the hopes they held for what was ahead.

In the weeks that followed, they were forced to wait it out and their nerves were strained with expectation. Elena and Elodie felt a sense of relief as the findings were finally revealed. Their grades, which demonstrated their diligence and willpower, were sufficient to get them into the universities of their choice. Even still, there was always a lingering sense of terror despite their achievement because they knew they would be leaving the comforts and familiarity of their shared adventure to face a vast unknown in strange nations.

As all of this was going on, Kian and Mike had started their own careers and were living lives that were now governed by their work schedules. With a startup, Kian was doing well in his role and was happy with the prospects and challenges it provided. Like him, Mike was happy in his position at a reputable company, and his income served as a concrete representation of his efforts and the new life he was starting.

The good news of Elodie and Elena's exam accomplishment brought happiness into their lives, even if they were physically separated. Kian and Mike, who had witnessed their friends work towards their objectives with steady determination and fortitude, were overcome with joy and pride when it was announced that they had been accepted into various colleges in various nations.

A sad reminder of the divergent directions their lives were taking was the reality that Elodie would be going to the UK and Elena to Germany. Despite their geographical distance from one another, their relationship remained strong and their lasting impact on each other's life was revealed, rather than diminishing their spirits.

As excited as she was about to move, Elena could not help but wish that the four of them could get together again. She cherished the dream of them all getting together again to celebrate their successes and enjoy the comfort of their friendship.

When they told Kian and Mike about their admittance, it sparked a conversation about the trip they had all done. Their lives had been a tapestry of common experiences, struggles, and victories, starting from the walls of their institution and continuing through the ordeals of exams and the transition into the employment. Kian and Mike were happy for Elena and Elodie's scholastic achievement, but they were also happy for the strength of their relationship, which remained constant despite their geographical separation and shifting circumstances.

Knowing that their friendship—which was tested in the harsh realities of university life and forged in the crucible of university life—would endure despite the constantly shifting circumstances, Elena prepared for her move to Germany and Elodie for her new life in the UK. Their future travels to other nations were not going to be the conclusion of their story; rather, they were going to be new chapters in a much bigger one, one that would carry on despite the distance between them.

The idea of going overseas to study and starting this new chapter in their life was both thrilling and intimidating. However, in the middle of this emotional tornado, Elena and Elodie stood bravely and optimistically on the edge of their futures with the unshakable support of Kian and Mike. No matter where their travels took them, their friendship, which served as a pillar of support in the shadow of uncertain new beginnings, assured them that their link would always be strong.

An atmosphere of excitement and melancholy farewells pervaded Elena's life as the pages flipped, her old academic days came to an end and a new journey abroad began. With Elodie, her constant companion on the path of learning and self-discovery, the final weeks before her departure were a whirlwind of exam preparation. They had done more than just complete their assignments; they had enrolled in a variety of worthwhile classes that broadened their horizons and helped them be ready for the challenging tests that were approaching.

And in the meantime, things had stabilised and Mike and Kian were finding fulfilment in their careers. Kian, who had moved into the corporate world with ease, was happy in his position at a startup that showed promise. Along with serving as evidence of his skill, his accomplishments also served as a ray of optimism for the future he and Elodie planned. Settled into the fast-paced world of a well-known corporation, Mike enjoyed the challenges and benefits that came with his work. It was evident from the decisions they had made after graduating from college that their careers were doing well.

Kian and Mike erupted in congrats upon hearing of Elena and Elodie's admittance into foreign colleges. Even with the digital media that now linked them geographically, they could still feel the delight. Elena hung onto the hope that they would be reunited before they left. Her heart had been set on seeing the four of them together. But as the days passed, it was clear that her dream of a reunion would never come true.

Her choice to spend the rest of her time with her family served as a painful reminder of the roots she was leaving behind, albeit briefly. A mixture of pride and worry was expressed by her parents, Carla and Miguel, as well as her younger brother Diego, whose worries of alienation mixed with their aspirations for her future. With a pledge ingrained in her heart, Elena vowed to herself that she would not let go of the things that bound her to her house, unlike her older sister Sofia.

The scene at the airport farewell was one of both excitement and melancholy. Elena felt the hollow emptiness of Mike's absence as she said goodbye to Elodie and watched her travel to the UK. To show his lover how much he loves him, only Kian showed up. In sharp contrast to the support Elena had hoped for in her last hours in South Africa, the tumultuous nature of their professional lives had kept them apart. The reunion that had been long-awaited and a ray of optimism amid all the disruptions was still only a pipe dream that melted into the whirlwind of life's continuous stream.

The friends Elena had anticipated would be there to say goodbye to her were not present at the busy airport on the day she left for her trip overseas. Her family was the only thing protecting her in the swarm of onlookers, their presence a reassuring constant amidst the whirlwind of her conflicting feelings. Elena had secretly hoped that Mike, who had been her biggest supporter during the many highs and lows of college life, would show up. His absence hurt, a mute monument to time's inexorable passage through life and its inevitable detours. Her family was comfortingly close by, but the absence of her friends, particularly Mike, cast a pall over her departure. Elena bore the burden of unsaid goodbyes and the knowledge that, in spite of their shared ties, each person was now navigating the seas of their own destiny, in addition to the luggage of her current journey, as she passed through the departure gates.

Realising that this was her new life started to set in as the plane took off and Elena was transported towards Hamburg. A lighthouse in the busy metropolis that offered fresh starts and challenges, the University of Hamburg waited. The sadness that accompanied the distances she now had from her loved ones was mixed with the thrill of travelling to a new nation and immersing herself in a new academic atmosphere and culture.

Elena set off with a mixture of nervousness and excitement on her search to make connections with new people in the strange halls of the University of Hamburg. Her friends' laughter and special experiences were jewels she carried with her, serving as a constant reminder of the relationships that had moulded her. However, there was a ray of light as she looked forward to making new friends and weaving fresh tales into the fabric of her life with the prospect of establishing new relationships.

Elena's transition to life was a tapestry of experiences, each day a stroke on the canvas of her new life. The city, with its rich history and vibrant culture, was a world waiting to be explored. The university, a melting pot of ideas and nationalities, offered endless opportunities for growth and learning. As she navigated the complexities of settling into her new environment, Elena found solace in the thought of her friends and family back home, their love a guiding light in her moments of solitude.

The story of Elena's voyage, which took her from the historic streets of South Africa to the sunny streets of Hamburg, was a monument to the strength of aspirations and the bravery required to follow them. It was a tale of closures and fresh starts, of partings and the hope of reunions. Elena understood the need to appreciate the past while welcoming the future and hold the memories while creating space for new ones as a result of her experiences. Her experience served as a reminder that, no matter where life leads us, what really defines us are the relationships, friendships, and love we have with one another.

Elena entered the next stage of her life in Hamburg with an open mind and an adventurous attitude, prepared to take on the pleasures and difficulties that awaited her. Her narrative was far from ended; it was only beginning to take shape, page by page, into an exciting future full of possibilities and optimism.

Chapter - 31
New Land, New Friends: Unveiling Paths

As Elena stepped onto the grounds of the University of Hamburg, she felt a surge of excitement mingled with a touch of apprehension. She was prepared to welcome this as a brand-new beginning and a new chapter in her life. She was welcomed by the colourful vitality and diverse cultural fabric of Hamburg, one of Germany's growing cities. But amidst the hustle and bustle, it was the roads of Germany, particularly the legendary Autobahn, that captured her imagination.

Elena was captivated by the Autobahn from the minute she stepped foot in Hamburg. It was nearly unbelievable to her that there could be a roadway with no speed limits. Driving on a road like that thrilled her as she is an avid auto enthusiast. But Elena was desperate to drive and feel the rush of racing down the Autobahn at fast speeds, even if other females might have been happy enough to be passengers.

She had always been unique due to her fascination with automobiles. Elena was engrossed in the world of cars and was eager to learn about every aspect, whereas others could have been uninterested or even hostile. She discovered joy and elegance in every facet of automotive culture, from the rumble of a powerful engine to the sleek lines of a sports car.

However, as Elena made her way around the halls of her new college, she concluded that her love of vehicles was not something that her friends shared. She tried her hardest to start conversations with her classmates, but in the first few days, she felt a little alone. But Elena was not one to be easily discouraged. She persisted in looking for chances to get in touch with people who had similar interests to her own with tenacity and resolve.

Elena's luck started to turn during one of these meetings. She was sitting in the university courtyard when she heard some students having a lively chat as she looked out over the busy crowds. She stepped closer to them, her pulse racing with eagerness as she summoned the bravery.

Finn, Chloe, and Luna were the three buddies that made up the gang. Warmth and companionship were radiating from Finn and Chloe, a pair deeply in love. Luna rounded out the group with her reflective eyes and calm manner. Elena was pulled to their magnetic aura despite her first misgivings.

Elena introduced herself, a timid grin laced with a tinge of anxiety in her voice. She was relieved that Finn, Chloe, and Luna welcomed her with a smile and made her feel comfortable with their kind demeanour. Elena felt a connection beginning to grow between them as they struck up a conversation.

Elena became close friends with Finn, Chloe, and Luna in the days that followed. They bonded over more than just casual connection as they exchanged stories and laughs. Their shared experiences as students navigating the challenges of university life gave them a common foundation despite their disparate backgrounds and interests.

Elena was incredibly happy and comforted by the bond she formed with Finn, Chloe, and Luna. She had long craved a sense of belonging, and she found it in their company. Spending time with them was always filled with love and laughter, whether they were strolling around Hamburg's streets or just relaxing in the university courtyard.

The presence of her new companions enhanced Elena's academic experience as the days stretched into weeks and the weeks into months. They had an abundance of adventures together and made memories that would last a lifetime. Every day they spent together became closer, from spontaneous road drives down the Autobahn to late-night study sessions spurred on by coffee and friendship.

But even in the middle of their jokes and friendship, Elena never forgot how much she loved vehicles. She continued to enjoy her love of automotive culture with Finn, Chloe, and Luna by her side. Her insatiable spirit of adventure was demonstrated by the fact that, despite the charm of Hamburg's streets, she was drawn to the open Autobahn.

Elena had found in Finn, Chloe, and Luna not just companions but also like-minded individuals who accepted her for who she was: a Spanish girl from South Africa with aspirational goals and an unquenchable thirst for exploration. Their connection acted as a lighthouse in a world full of limitless opportunities as they navigated the meandering paths of college life together.

When Elena thought back on her journey, she realised that the friendships she had made along the road would be just as important to her as her academic accomplishments during her time at the University of Hamburg. And she was full of excitement and expectation as she looked to the future, knowing that she would have no shortage of possibilities and adventures along the way.

A tapestry of newly formed friendships, exciting late-night excursions, and the quest for freedom started to take shape as the days passed. Her relationships with Finn, Chloe, and Luna grew stronger; they went from being hesitant bonds in the beginning to a firm base of encouragement, companionship, and shared experiences. The four of them, each with a unique narrative to tell, discovered a sense of community in one another that went beyond the typical boundaries of friendship. With Finn driving his compact car, their late-night travels turned into a much-loved tradition. Their chats, their dreams, and the laughter that permeated the air were all witnessed by the streets of Hamburg, softly lit by streetlights. Despite being straightforward, these encounters had a certain enchantment that attested to the happiness that comes from friendship.

Elena noticed that she was becoming more and more attached to her new acquaintances as she continued to be completely honest with them. She loved spending time with Finn, Chloe, and Luna because she had a genuine connection with them all, which was both a gift and a vulnerability. The separation that had developed between her and her former companions, Mike, Elodie, and Kian, remained, nevertheless, even amid her newfound happiness. The ensuing stillness between them troubled her much, even though she knew the responsibilities of their lives. She felt a mixture of nostalgia and grief as she recalled their time together and the unbreakable link they had previously had. Elena clung to the belief that their bond would withstand time and distance, even despite their hectic lifestyles.

Elena accepted the duties of adulthood with grace and tenacity as she pursued independence. She worked as a home tutor in the evenings, which not only allowed her to support herself financially but also to share her knowledge and love of learning. Despite its challenges, this experience was extremely fulfilling for her, giving her a feeling of purpose and the satisfaction of seeing her kids grow and develop. Elena's work at the workplace represented her ideals and her dedication to hard work and independence; it was more than simply a means to an end.

Elena took a step towards actual freedom when she chose to live alone in an apartment. She could ponder on her voyage and face the loneliness that occasionally crept into the solitude of her own place, which served as both a challenge and a haven. Elena welcomed a dog named Julie into her life as a way to break the silence. Elena's world was made even more joyful and comforting by Julie's presence. Elena found comfort and joy in her pet's unconditional affection, the thrill of meeting her at the door, and the simple joy of their walks together. Beyond being merely a pet, Julie served as a source of happiness and a reminder of the small pleasures in life, especially during times when the darkness of loneliness was beginning to overshadow people.

Keeping a balance between her work, her education, and her time with Julie became part of Elena's everyday routine. Her university classes were a constant source of challenge, one that she approached with zest and determination. Her mornings were devoted to pursuing academic achievement. Her drive for learning and her desire for success were fueled by the cerebral stimulation and the sense of accomplishment that accompanied grasping new ideas.

Her apartment was no longer the place she spent her evenings alone; instead, her tutoring sessions brought her laughter and warmth. Reward in and of itself was the joy she felt from seeing her pupils' lightbulb moments and assisting them in comprehending difficult subjects. Through her role, Elena was able to positively impact others' lives, though in a tiny way.

Julie's presence changed her nights, which used to be the worst time of her day. Elena found relief from the worries of her day when she arrived home to her animal companion's eager devotion and wagging tail. Feeding Julie, playing with her, and falling asleep with the dog snuggled up by her side became routines that she looked forward to and treasured, serving as a constant reminder of the value of caring for herself and others.

Elena persevered and kept an open mind to the opportunities ahead as she managed the challenges of her new life in Hamburg. Her experience served as a tribute to the strength of friendship, the importance of perseverance, and the unconditional love that animals can offer. Elena discovered a rhythm that was all her own in juggling her work, her education, and her relationship with Julie. This rhythm gave her hope, tenacity, and an unyielding spirit of adventure as she faced each new day.

One fine day, Elena was excited to see her friends Finn, Chloe, and Luna as soon as she set foot on the university premises. Their friendship had grown to be an essential part of her time at university, providing her with much-needed stability in the large and occasionally daunting world of academia. Her steps sped in anticipation as they got closer to their regular meeting place; she was excited to laugh and tell stories, just like they had done numerous times before. But today there was something new in the picture, a stranger among the known faces.

Elena was drawn in by the girl named Kelly who stood a little apart but blended in with the group in an unidentified manner. Elena greeted Kelly with the warm smile that had always marked her approach and an open heart. Kelly returned the favour. Kelly's smile and her easy-going manner conveyed that she was more than just a passing acquaintance to Finn, Chloe, and Luna. Although their first conversation was characterised by the polite but slightly pretentious small talk that characterises first encounters, Elena couldn't help but be captivated by this newcomer to their group. What tales did Kelly bring to this close-knit community, and who was she? Elena's thoughts was full with questions, her innate desire for connection and friendship stoking the possibility of new relationships being forged.

At first, Kelly's arrival in her social group appeared to be a natural progression of her growing sense of belonging, a chance to expand the group that had grown to be her second home. However, there was a subtle shift in the dynamics of the group, something Elena saw but believed would pass with time.

Elena greeted Kelly with her customary warmth and openness as soon as she joined the group, showing her willingness to make connections and develop friendships. They had a friendly first exchange, with both of them smiling and exchanging pleasantries. But Elena couldn't shake a nagging feeling of dread, a whisper of intuition suggesting their group's equilibrium might be in jeopardy.

The next day, Kelly's behaviour towards Elena took an odd turn, which made this emotion much more intense. Elena was starting to feel uneasy because of Kelly's strange glance in her direction. Elena tried to brush these thoughts off as a simple misunderstanding, but Kelly's inconsistent behaviour—alternating between forced grins and icy indifference—added more layers of uncertainty to her already conflicted feelings.

The ties that had seemed unshakable started to show symptoms of strain as the days went by. Elena felt as though the close-knit group that had served as her compass in the huge sea of academic life was eroding due to currents that she was unable to fully comprehend. Instead of being abrupt, the gap developed over time, slowly eroding the companionship that had once characterised their partnership. Once so much a part of Elena's everyday existence, Finn, Chloe, and Luna started to fade away, their interactions with her less regular and more ceremonial.

It broke Elena's heart to realise that her pals were now hanging out without her, going on late-night drives and dinners that they had used to share. She had been glaringly absent from these outings that had formerly been the highlight of her days, full of friendship and laughing. She was very aware of the growing distance between herself and the individuals she had come to regard as her second family, and the agony of this exclusion was intense with each incident.

A deep sense of loneliness now clouded nights that had formerly been filled with the promise of experiences to be shared. Elena struggled with thoughts of desertion, and her once-vibrant social life was reduced to quiet evenings spent with Julie, her devoted dog. She found some comfort in the unconditional affection of her pet, but it was unable to erase the ingrained sense of loneliness that had crept into her heart.

This social seclusion had a significant effect on Elena. She started to feel more and more depressed and anxious instead of the joy and self-assurance that had formerly defined her. The heavy weight of loneliness was something that came with every day and appeared to get heavier as time went on. The institution, which had previously been a hub of potential and enthusiasm, had transformed into an uncertain environment where doubt and uneasiness were pervasive.

It hurt all the time to see how different her life was now from the carefree days she used to spend with Finn, Chloe, and Luna. It was difficult to accept that Kelly's presence might be the primary cause of the group's shifting dynamics. Elena was plagued by the mystery of why and how the presence of a single person could cause their friendship to fall apart; it felt like a puzzle with pieces that were just out of reach.

Elena noticed that she was becoming more and more reclusive as she tried to get through this turbulent time. There was a veil of reflection and melancholy over the previously lively and gregarious student who had embraced university life with great enthusiasm. Her desire to succeed academically was tempered by her personal struggles, which had previously inspired and motivated her. Instead, it became a chore to be completed.

During her lonely moments, Elena thought about how relationships are brittle and the complex interplay of people's personalities and situations that might bring them closer or break them. During this time, she learned the value of independence and the fortitude that comes from taking on challenges head-on. These were tough but priceless lessons.

Elena was determined to make her way through the emotional maze that had captured her, despite the sorrow and difficulties she faced. She looked ahead with cautious optimism, Julie by her side and the will to get her happiness back. Elena was prepared to confront the unknown with confidence, motivated by the knowledge of her past experiences and the expectation of better times ahead. The road ahead was loaded with opportunities for development as well as potential hazards.

Chapter - 32
Journeys of Elena DeSanta: A Tale of Dreams and Destinies

Elena's time at the University of Hamburg had become increasingly isolated. She decided to make a place for herself, free from the complications and disappointments of failed relationships, after having disturbing experiences with her friends. She had to walk carefully around the campus, which had once seemed to be a place full of opportunities for new experiences and connections, since she was afraid of the hurt that too frequently seemed to come with getting too near.

She did not come to the choice to cut ties with those she considered to be poisonous lightly. Elena has always appreciated the warmth and depth of friendship, the happiness that comes from spending time together, and the support that comes from one another. But the way things had been going of late had her doubting even the basis of these relationships. She had been deeply wounded by the betrayal and marginalisation by those she thought were close to her, and the uncertainty of being alone had become more alluring to her than the possibility of friendship.

Elena took comfort in her work as a home instructor in the stillness of her self-imposed seclusion. She found a sense of purpose and fulfilment in helping youngsters understand difficult topics and in seeing their moments of growth and understanding that she had not yet experienced in her university life. Her broken spirit was soothed by these meetings, which were a far cry from the drama of her peer relationships and a reminder that she could have a beneficial influence on other people's lives.

Another comfort during this difficult time was Julie, her devoted dog. Her four-legged pet provided her with peaceful companionship on the nights that used to be filled with the laughing and chatter of friends. Julie was a continuous reminder that loyalty and love could take many different shapes because of her everlasting devotion and her excited greeting at the door each evening. Elena discovered a tranquilly that had grown more elusive among her human companions as she cuddled with Julie, experiencing the warmth and unconditional affection of her pet.

Luna's invitation caught her off guard because of this atmosphere of reflection and isolation. The idea of getting back on the road late at night with her friends caused Elena to feel a range of emotions after what seemed like an eternity spent managing her days by herself. Even though she was still dealing with the pain and confusion of the previous several months, the mere act of being remembered and included gave her a glimmer of hope.

Elena was asked to step back from the barriers she had erected around herself, and she accepted the invitation with warmth and what appeared to be sincere intent. It was possible that all was not lost because Luna, Finn, Chloe, and even Kelly were willing to reach out and close the distance that had grown. The idea of making amends and reigniting the friendship that had previously characterised their group was thrilling and terrifying at the same time.

Elena came up with an idea that directly addressed her love of vehicles, which she intended to share with her friends as a show of kindness and reconciliation, in an effort to heal the brittle strands of friendship. This goal in mind, she headed to a nearby car rental, her eyes focused on locating the ideal car for an unexpected gift that she thought would mend their damaged relationship. Each car glistened in the showroom lights, beckoning freedom and adventure, and the rental lot was an exhibition of diverse automobiles. She passed by several of them, but none of them seemed to understand her intentions until she fixed her eyes on a BMW M5 CS. A beacon amidst the sea of possibilities, it stood out with its forceful attitude and sleek lines that called out to her.

Elena chose to rent a BMW because she wanted to make amends and revive the friendship that had waned over the previous few months. This wasn't a spur-of-the-moment decision. Elena found herself wandering the vast campus of the University of Hamburg, her daily experiences serving as a reminder of the connections that she so desperately wanted to heal. She was becoming less and less insistent about keeping her distance from people who she believed had harmed her, and more and more hopeful that maybe a big gesture could heal the rift that had been created.

The hours before the scheduled drive passed in a whirl of planning and second-guessing. There was a jittery atmosphere in Elena's flat, which had once been a place of isolation and introspection. Being aware of her owner's emotional struggle, Julie continued to be a reassuring presence, providing Elena with silent company that eased her fraying nerves. The city of Hamburg changed as night fell, with the gloom broken by the brightness of streetlights and the distant sound of traffic.

Elena stretched out to Luna, her heart pounding in her chest as she dialled the number, the BMW parked outside, a horse waiting for its moment of glory. The call was unexpectedly devastating, as she was met with a brusque reaction and a swift hang-up. Rejection hurt like hell, reminding her deep down of the danger she was putting herself in. She wasn't deterred and tried to get in touch with Finn and Chloe, but she was faced with the same dismissals. Every conversation she had was another brick in the wall of loneliness she had been attempting, valiantly, to bring down.

Her last hope, Kelly, picked up the phone. Elena felt a brief sense of relief upon hearing her voice, but it was fleeting. It hit her in the gut to hear that the drive had already started without her. It felt like a monument to her ignorance, the BMW that had once been a light of promise. It hurt so much to be alone and to know that all of her hard work and sacrifice had been for nothing.

Elena withdrew to the safety of her flat and sought comfort in Julie's unflinching love. Seeing that her owner was upset, the dog quietly comforted her, her presence a constant amidst Elena's chaos. And then the tears began, an unending cascade of grief and annoyance. Each sob is a witness to the intensity of her involvement in these relationships and the painful reality of their fragility; the betrayal, genuine or perceived, wounded deep.

Elena's night of tears was a cathartic release, a purging of the hopes and expectations that had been dashed so cruelly. As dawn broke over Hamburg, the light creeping into her apartment brought with it a sense of clarity. The journey ahead would be hers alone to navigate, a path of self-discovery and independence that no longer hinged on the acceptance or approval of others. In the quiet aftermath of her heartbreak, Elena found a resolve she hadn't known she possessed, a determination to forge ahead and find joy in her own company and in the passions that had always fueled her spirit.

Elena's life changed as a result of this reflective time. It was freeing to realise that she was happy regardless of the whims and affections of other people. Like the Autobahn she had previously fantasised about navigating, the road ahead seemed unbounded and wide. Elena went into the day with a renewed sense of purpose and hope, with Julie by her side and a bright future ahead. With an optimistic spirit, she was prepared to welcome the trip ahead with open arms, knowing that the lessons learnt would help her navigate the scars of the past and heal in due course.

Elena's decision to drive into the night by herself, with a cigarette burning in one hand while she drove the rented BMW with the other, was a crucial time of self-reflection and unadulterated emotion. The car was moving towards Berlin on the A24 Autobahn when the darkness descended, the roar of the powerful engine a sharp contrast to the agitation roiling inside her. The headlights of the car cut through the darkness, illuminating the road ahead and reflecting the clarity she was seeking amidst the jumble of her feelings and ideas.

The miles passed quickly, and Elena found herself in a solitary haven where she could face the rush of memories and ideas that were filling her head. The soundtrack to the turbulent story of her life was a blend of lively and eerie songs that played in the background. She felt a tide of memories rush over her with every song, each one stinging with regret or anguish or nostalgia.

A twinge of sadness came when she remembered her grandparents, who had died when she was only entering adolescence. During her early years, they had been her pillars of support, providing her with unwavering love and guidance. Time appeared to never be able to heal the emptiness left by their departure, which served as a continual reminder of how fleeting life is and how inevitable loss is.

Her elder sister Sofia, with whom she had become alienated, was another source of family conflict. Elena had been deeply upset by Sofia's decision to break her ties to the family and pursue her life in the United States. Her family dynamics were characterised by a complicated web of relationships, as evidenced by the gulf of unanswered questions and unresolved emotions that spanned the quiet between them.

The ghosts of her previous relationships—with Jake and Peter—rose from the recesses of her consciousness, their recollections tinged with happy times marred by hurt and betrayal. Elena let out her fury and rage into the emptiness, releasing the pent-up anger that was beneath her calm demeanour. She struggled to accept the fact that love, in all of its manifestations, had frequently left her more shattered than whole.

Her best buddy Mike, who had been a constant in her life, seemed to be fading into the distance. Whether by choice or by circumstance, his absence from her in her hour of need was a wound that would not heal. The overwhelming sense of loneliness that descended upon her served as a sharp reminder of the gaps that had developed between them—distances expressed not in kilometres but rather in lost chances for companionship and assistance.

"Why God, why me?" Absorbing by the noise of the engine and the rush of the wind, the query tore from her lips and appeared to echo into the night. She was faced with her struggles and had a period of existential reflection during which she questioned the fairness of how happiness and suffering are distributed in life.

Elena's mind drifted to her family as the Autobahn opened up in front of her, a ribbon of opportunity leading to an unknowable destination. Love was what kept them together, no matter how complicated their relationships were. The two people who had always given her the most support and love were her parents, Carla and Miguel. Their expectations had put her under a lot of strain.

A ray of innocence and hope in Elena's turbulent life was her younger brother Diego, who was finishing his last year of education. His hopes and aspirations served as a reminder of the value of familial ties and the possibility of progress and atonement because they were untarnished by the harsh realities that had clouded her own perception.

An exploration of oneself turned into the drive into the night, which had begun as a way to get away from the hurt of loneliness and rejection. Elena shaved off layers of grief, disappointment, and rage with every mile, revealing the essence of her being—a soul that yearned for love, acceptance, and connection.

The night's calm was broken by the abrupt ring of her phone. She recognised the caller as Carla, her mother. Elena paused, considering whether or not to answer the call. She was aware that her mother would only give her a call at this late hour if it was an emergency. She was aware, however, that it was risky to answer a phone call while operating a vehicle.

But Elena was unable to ignore her mother's call when she called again. She took up the phone, attempting to focus her gaze on the road while she spoke. She was distracted for only a short second, though, and her automobile drifted into the right lane, crashing at 240 km/h into a truck.

The crash had a catastrophic effect. Elena was bleeding profusely from her arms and head, and her automobile was completely wrecked on the right side. On the phone, she could hear her mother's terrified voice, but she was too sick to speak. In a desperate attempt to inform her mother that she was in an accident, she reached for her phone, which had fallen close to her leg.

Elena's mind raced with ideas as she fumbled to get to her phone. She considered how careful she had always been behind the wheel and how one slip-up could endanger her life. She also thought about Julie, her dog, and how dearly she was adored. She couldn't bear the thought of leaving Julie behind as she was her sole friend in Germany.

At last, Elena was able to retrieve her phone and noticed that Julie's picture was her wallpaper. Looking at her pet dog's image brought her calm despite the shock and anguish. Before she died, she closed her eyes and pleaded to God to take care of Julie.

Elena, 24, was full of bright hopes and dreams on the eve of a terrible day; she had no idea that these would be abruptly cut off. Elena was the epitome of youthful vigour and drive, navigating the difficulties of life with a passion that was as contagious as it was inspirational. Her wide-ranging and diverse dreams extended beyond the comfortable walls of her German apartment and reached the continents, all the way back to her South African family's home. The only people who really understood the depth of her heart and the scope of her goals were her family, for whom she served as a light of love and hope.

The Autobahn has a reputation for being dangerous because of its unrestricted speeds, which frequently result in disastrous consequences. It is well-known for its expansive networks that connect the vast regions of Germany. Elena's voyage came to an abrupt end as fate took a terrible turn on this same path. The young dreamer's ambitions were crushed by an abrupt and cruel car accident that left a quiet where there had once been joy, ambition, and hopes for an unrealized future.

Elena left behind those whose lives were affected by her absence in the wake of the catastrophe. Tucked away in the warmth of South Africa, her family struggled with a loss so great that it appeared to overshadow the brightness that beamed over their house. Julie waited patiently in the solitude of her German apartment, miles away, awaiting a return that would never come. Elena was a young, vibrant person, and her passing is a heartbreaking reminder of how fleeting life is and how unpredictable fate can be, particularly when travelling on the Autobahn where things can change drastically in an instant.

With a loss too great to put into words, Elena's family took comfort in recollections of a daughter and sister whose laughter had once warmed their home. As a memorial to the life she had lived, however short, they held to the struggles of her dreams, to the plans and hopes she had entertained. Despite their grief, they were able to draw strength from one another and show a collective fortitude that paid up to Elena's legacy of love and close family ties.

Elena's loyal companion Julie, who stayed behind, came to represent Elena's unwavering spirit in Germany. The puppy gave Elena a physical link and served as a constant reminder of the unconditional affection and small pleasures that characterise our interactions with the people and animals we love. The essence of Elena's love was conveyed by Julie's eager eyes and bouncing tail; her legacy of companionship and kindness persisted even after she passed away.

Even though Elena's narrative was cruelly cut short, it left a legacy of dreams unbowed by hardship and a love that aimed to mend broken hearts. It's an appeal to everyone who knew her, including those who only know her via the echoes of her story, to live life to the fullest, love unconditionally, and walk gently on the planet while keeping in mind the legacy we hope to leave behind.

Elena DeSanta, one that was intertwined with themes of fervently pursuing aspirations, treasured and lost connections, and the sadness of sudden goodbyes. Elena's voyage, which takes her from the colourful streets of Soweto to the melancholy silence of Hamburg, perfectly captures the feeling of teenage ambition colliding with the unexpected decisions of fate. Her journey inspires us to consider our own lives, as it is characterised by the quest for independence, the warmth of relationships that are made and broken, and the sobering realisation of life's frailty. Elena DeStana left a legacy that serves as a mirror, teaching us the value of living in the present, fostering our connections, and approaching life's open road with optimism and fortitude—even when we don't know where it will go.\